Dedication

Brad Bowling dedicates his work on this book to Joanne Forbus, Cindy Moore, Jennifer Moore, Gertrude Haughton, Jon Forbus, Wanda Nesbit, Theresa Glenn, Louis Rowles, Kay Moffett, Janice Beatty, Robin Nivens, Larry Marett, Peggy Holmes, Ruth Griffith, Linda Herndon, Gaylynn Cantrell, Brenda Pearson, and all of the other underpaid, underappreciated, and undervalued teachers of America. There's no rational explanation for why they choose this profession, but we all benefit from their work.

Authors' Bios

Brad Bowling has been writing about and photographing Mustangs since 1985. He has been the editor of *Mustang Times*, public relations coordinator for Saleen Autosport, associate editor of *Mustang Illustrated*, editor of *Old Cars Weekly*, and director of Web site development for Charlotte Motor Speedway. The author of 11 automotive books, Bowling lives with his wife Heather and their American Eskimo in Concord, N.C.

Jerry Heasley is a long, tall Texan from the panhandle town of Pampa. He drives a real 1965 289 Cobra roadster and has written 10 books about Mustangs, plus more than 3,600 magazine articles on muscle and performance cars. He has spent the last 20 years building and maintaining one of the largest private collections of car pictures in the world.

Contents

Dedication 3
Authors' Bios 3
Contents 4
Acknowledgments 6
About the Photos in this Book 6
Introduction 7

SECTION 1.   INDY PACE CARS p. 8

    1964-1/2 Indy Pace Car Replica 9
    1979 Indy Pace Car Replica 12
    1994 Indy Pace Car Replica 15

SECTION 2.   NATIONAL PROMOTIONS p. 18

    1966-68 Springtime Sprint 19
    1971 Special Value Package 23
    1972 Sprint Editions 25
    1995 GTS 28

SECTION 3.   REGIONAL PROMOTIONS p. 30

    1966-68 High Country Special 31
    1967 Lone Star Limited 36
    1967 Ski Country Special 38
    1967 Indy Pacesetter 39
    1968 California Special 40
    1968 Golden Nugget Special 43
    1968 Cardinal Edition 44
    1969 Limited Edition 600 45
    1970 ARI/Twister Specials 48
    1970 Sidewinder Special 51
    1985 Twister II 52
    1987 Ford Motorsport Nationals Special Edition 54
    1989 Carolina Ford Dealers 56

SECTION 4.   DEALERSHIP PROMOTIONS p. 59

    1967 Stallion 60
    1989 M-25 Kansas City 62

SECTION 5.   PRETTY COLORS p. 64

    1966 One Millionth Anniversary Gold 65
    1967 Playboy Pink 66
    1968 Colors of the Month 68

SECTION 5. (cont.)   PRETTY COLORS

- 1968-69 Rainbow of Colors 70
- 1970 Grabber 71
- 1996 SVT Cobra Mystic 72
- 2004 SVT Cobra Mystichrome 75

SECTION 6.   HAPPY ANNIVERSARY p. 77

- 1984 20th Anniversary GT-350 78
- 1993 Saleen SA-10 81
- 1998 Saleen SA-15 83
- 1999 35th Anniversary Mustang 85
- 2003 Centennial Mustang 87
- 2003 Cobra 10th Anniversary 89
- 2003 Saleen SA-20 92
- 2004 40th Anniversary Mustang 95

SECTION 7.   HARD-CHARGING PERFORMANCE SPECIALS p. 97

- 1965 Shelby GT-350R 98
- 1966 Shelby GT-350H 102
- 1978 Mustang II King Cobra 105
- 1985-1/2 SVO Comp Prep 109
- 1989 Saleen SSC 113
- 1990-93 Saleen SC 117
- 1992-93 SAAC Mk I, Mk II, and Snake 120
- 1993 SVT Cobra R 123
- 1994 Saleen SR 127
- 1995 SVT Cobra R 130
- 2000 SVT Cobra R 134
- 2003 Roush Boyd Coddington California Roadster 137

SECTION 8.   FOX LIMITED EDITIONS p. 139

- 1990 Limited Edition 140
- 1992-1/2 Limited Edition 142
- 1993 Limited Edition 144

SECTION 9.   MOVIE TIE-INS p. 146

- 2001 Bullitt 147
- 2003 Saleen "Hollywood Horsepower" 150

SECTION 10.   THE FUTURE LOOKS BRIGHT! p. 152

- 2006 SVT GT-500 153
- 2006 Stallion 156

Acknowledgments

Jerry and I owe a debt of gratitude to several people who helped make this ambitious undertaking less scary.

My local club, the ever-helpful **Carolina Regional Mustang Club**, of Charlotte, N.C., has always been a source of fine, restored photo subjects. Because of the specialized nature of this book, only a few club cars are used for illustration, but to view even more gorgeous Mustangs from the Carolina group, visit the club's Web site at www.ponytales.org. I especially want to thank Dave Goff and Norm Demers for patiently answering my unending stream of questions.

One of my favorite places to visit in Concord, N.C., is **Morrison Motor Co.**, which is owned by Jimmy Morrison. Jimmy and I have spent many an hour deep in car-guy talk during the past 10 years, and there's always something on his lot that I really want to take home. Corvettes, Firebirds/Camaros, Vipers, Impalas, Jeeps, and Prowlers abound—always sprinkled liberally with Mustang GTs, Saleens, and SVT Cobras. In addition to the company's inventory, Jimmy's huge private collection includes a '71 Mach 1 with 429-cid power, a '69 Boss 302, a '69 GT coupe sporting a 428-cid V-8, and two never-driven '93 SVT Cobras. Morrison Motor Co.'s main lot is located at 1170 Old Charlotte Road, Concord, NC 28027. The phone number is (704) 782-7716, and the Web site is www.morrisonmotorco.com.

Daniel Carpenter is one of the most avid collectors of low-mileage, late-model Mustangs in the country, and he specializes in the 1979-93 Fox period. His personal collection includes a '79 Pace Car Replica, '83 convertible, two '86 GTs, and a '93 SVT Cobra R—none of which have ever been driven! Additionally, there is a low-mile '89 GT, a 3,000-mile '93 LX convertible, and a couple of Cobras running around his place with less than 4,000 miles each. Daniel was nice enough to prep the cars I needed for my photography so these largely unseen treasures could be shared with the readers of this book. Daniel is the son of Dennis Carpenter—the famous reproducer of impossible-to-find Ford parts. Daniel's shop, which sits just down the street from his father's place, turns out rubber and plastic reproduction Mustang parts, often from original Ford factory molds. For information about the Mustang components his company produces, contact Daniel Carpenter Reproductions at 4310 Concord Parkway S., Concord, NC 28027 or (704) 786-0990.

It was through Daniel Carpenter that I met **Monty Seawright**, the only person I know whose enthusiasm for 1979-present Mustangs has resulted in a 30-plus collection of low-mileage beauties. Monty endured some hot summer days with unbelievable patience as I shot many of his cars for this book and many other projects.

Greg Wackett was instrumental in tracking down information and cars for the Saleen chapters. Greg has let me borrow tons of material from his Saleen archives, and he seems to know everybody who ever thought about buying one of the California-built high-performance Mustangs. He can be reached through saleenlocator@yahoo.com.

Mark LaMaskin is another expert who buys and sells Saleen Mustangs and SVT Cobras for a living through Performance Autosport (www.performanceautosport.com). Mark has welcomed me to his shop in Richmond, Va., many times to shoot his inventory; he's another collector who will gladly hand me a dealer license plate and a set of keys to a 300-horsepower supercharged Mustang with no questions asked. Mark can be reached at Performance Autosport, 12927 Plaza Dr., Ste. B, Richmond, VA 23233 and (804) 784-8851 or through info@performanceautosport.com.

I met **Don Hughmanick** through his Web site while doing research for this book. Don owns a 1969 Limited 600 Mustang (pictured in this book) and has accumulated quite a bit of information about that special pony and other regional and national Ford promotions. Visit his site at www.limited600mustang.com.

When we needed SVO information, we went to **Matt Walker**, who straightened us out about the rare Competition Preparation models produced during 1984-86.

- Brad Bowling
October, 2005

About the Photos in this Book

Preparing a photo book about limited edition Mustangs can be as frustrating as doing the same for Bigfoot or alien visitors. We found it was often the case that there were no surviving examples to capture with our digital cameras, so a few chapters of this book must get by with a scratchy vintage snapshot, or worse—no picture at all!

Most images in *Mustang Specials* were taken by authors Brad Bowling and Jerry Heasley, but you will also see credited pictures from Don Hughmanick, Ford Motor Company, Saleen Inc., Peter Sessler, and David Charlier.

Introduction

What is a Special Edition Mustang?

The authors tried to establish several solid criteria for determining which cars would be included in this book about special edition Mustangs. Some were easy choices—the 1968 California Special and High Country Special quickly went to the top of the list. Others were cause for debate: the '65 Shelby GT-350R and certain Saleen and Roush models, for example.

It's not that we liked or disliked some Mustangs more than others, but we had to eliminate models that were certainly "special" in some ways but could not truly be considered special editions. The '71 Mach 1 with a 429-cid Super Cobra Jet V-8 is obviously a hot car (and more rare than some models Ford labeled "limited editions") but we deemed it to be a production model (Mach 1) built with an optional factory engine.

Our guidelines for adding to or eliminating from the list read something like this:

- A special edition is an offshoot of a regular production model.
- A special edition is not offered year after year.
- Intent plays a role in special edition status. Did Ford intend to create a new model when it introduced the California Special, or was it a one-time-only proposition?
- Does the special edition in question have any historical significance? Another way to phrase this is: In hindsight, does this model stand out from the crowd?
- How did the target audience respond to the package?
- Shelbys, Saleens, SVOs, SVTs, and Roushes are to be treated as production models, but anything that deviates from their established formats in limited numbers can be considered a special edition.

Were we able to include every regional or dealer promotion in this book? No, obviously there are many of these cars still waiting to be discovered out there. And don't even think about finding an entry for every Mustang with special order paint in here. That's the kind of in-depth research that Tony Popish has performed through his *Horse of a Different Color* registry and newsletter; it would take a 300-page volume just to discuss all of his findings.

What should you do if there is a Mustang in your driveway or garage with unusual markings or features that might indicate a promotional package? First, enjoy driving it. Second, surf the Internet for online registries that know something about your car. Failing that, create your own Web registry so people can start coming to you with information.

We hope you enjoy this book and learn more about some oddball entries in the 40-year history of the Ford Mustang.

SECTION 1:

Indianapolis 500 Pace Car Replicas

From its first running in 1911, the annual Indianapolis 500 has held the attention of racing enthusiasts from around the world and is considered "The Greatest Spectacle in Racing" by many.

When founding Indy father Carl G. Fisher proposed the inaugural race begin with a rolling start—partly for safety, partly for pageant—he accidentally created the sponsor-friendly phenomenon of the production-based pace car. No fool Fisher, pacing privileges were initially doled to Stoddard-Dayton models (1911, 1913, and 1914) from his own Indianapolis dealership. Later, long-gone manufacturers such as Packard, Marmon, H.C.S, National Sextet, Duesenberg, Cole, and Rickenbacker received national attention that one day a year when their newest V-8, V-12, or V-16 led the pack around the 2.5-mile superspeedway.

As the sport evolved, so did the role of the pace car. Before the 1970s pace cars tended to be the top performance model of the participating company—unmodified but for colorful graphics declaring their special status in the festival of speed. Once television exposed every American household to the Indy race, automakers started selling pace car replicas to the public.

Early 1970s production vehicles—with their detuned, asthmatic engines—required custom-built powerplants, modified brakes, and stiffer-than-stock suspensions before taking on pace car duty. The death of the factory-built American convertible gave birth to some innovative roof-chopping ideas, and automakers struggled to create viable open bodies from their existing stock. In 1979, IMS officials added caution-lap duty to the pace car's role, which meant raising the performance bar for any submitted vehicle.

The Mustang has valiantly served as pace car for the Indianapolis 500 three times, and the Ford Motor Company produced and marketed a highly visible series of replicas in each year.

Indy Pace Car Replica

1964-1/2

photo car owned by Drew Takach

When Ford debuted the Mustang on April 17, 1964, as an early 1965 model it combined sporty looks, economical operation (in base equipment form), and brisk performance for a price any working American could afford.

Part of the car's huge appeal was its ability to be ordered as a well-equipped "stripper" all the way to a luxury sports car. With its long hood, short deck, sculptured sides, and sporty bucket seats the Mustang was perfect for a single owner, newlywed couple, young family, or empty-nesters who yearned for a taste of youthful exuberance.

Initially available only in coupe and convertible form, the new pony gained a 2+2 fastback body style around the true start of the '65 model year. All three were built on a 108-inch wheelbase, measured 181.6 inches from chromed bumper to chromed bumper, and weighed between 2,449 (hardtop) and 2,615 pounds (convertible). At $2,368 nicely appointed, the Mustang was comparable to, or cheaper than, its main rivals: Chevrolet's Corvair Monza Spyder coupe ($2,599), Spyder convertible ($2,811), and Plymouth's Barracuda fastback ($2,365).

The Mustang's standard powerplant was a U-code 170-cid inline-six (with 101 horsepower), which was admittedly weak compared to its competition: Corvair's flat-six (150) and Barracuda's "slant" six (145), but Ford's line of optional V-8s more than made up for the deficit. The initial F-code 260-cid V-8 with two-barrel produced 164 horsepower, but it was replaced within the first six months by the D-code 289 four-barrel V-8 (210 horsepower) and legendary high-performance K-code 289 (271 horsepower) with solid lifters.

Ford marketers commandeered the population wave of post-war Baby Boomers by labeling them the "Mustang Generation." Although April 17 marked the car's first sales date, Ford's publicity machine created a pre-release buzz the likes of which had never been felt in Detroit. All three television networks ran commercials for their 29 million viewers the night before the debut—there were even advertisements beforehand to let people know to watch for the commercials—and spectators at the New York World's Fair were treated to a special display and unveiling ceremony. More than 22,000 orders were recorded at Ford dealerships that first day, and sales reached 417,000 within 12 months. With only a half year on the market before the start of the '65 model season, Mustang sold 120,000 units, putting it behind only a handful of established people-movers from Chevrolet (Impala, Bel Air, and Chevelle) and Ford (Galaxie 500). To fill dealer orders, Ford began pumping ponies out of its Dearborn, Mich.; San Jose, Calif.; and Metuchen, N.J., plants.

Thanks to a strong economy, most first-year Mustangs were ordered well equipped, and only 27 percent had the six-cylinder engine. Nearly half had automatic transmissions and 20 percent were built with the extra-cost four-speed manual.

On May 30, just six weeks after the Mustang's official launch, several convertibles served as pace and "festival" cars at the 48th running of the Indianapolis 500. Three race-duty convertibles were modified by North Carolina NASCAR shop Holman-Moody with 271-horsepower K-code V-8s, four-speed Borg-Warner transmissions, and stiffer, lower suspension components to handle the 2.5-mile track. The three droptops were Wimbledon White (paint code M), and their whereabouts today are unknown.

Thirty-five "festival" cars were used by various

The owners of this replica did a great job of chasing parts and learning the history of their pace car while restoring it. *(Brad Bowling)*

The owners of this restored 1964-1/2 pace car replica drive their Mustang nearly every day. *(Brad Bowling)*

Contrary to legend, the production pace car replicas were not built with the K-code (271-horse) V-8, but with this 164-horse F-code 260. *(Brad Bowling)*

The owners of this Mustang had pace car graphics designed and applied from old photos and Ford's specifications. *(Brad Bowling)*

dignitaries and staff of the track in association with the famous Memorial Day Sunday race, all convertibles plucked from the Dearborn assembly line with no clear mandate about equipment except engine (D-code 289/four-barrel) and color (Wimbledon White). The festival cars' graphics package differed from the coupes in that the blue striping was applied to the tail lamp panel, hubcaps wore spinners, and driver-side mirrors were installed. The convertibles were sent to auction after the race, but only one has been located.

On learning that his new Mustang had been chosen for pace car duty Lee Iacocca created a "Checkered Flag" competition among Ford dealers wherein the most successful sellers would attend a special dinner and receive keys to a pace car replica. Separate "Green Flag" contest winners picked up their replicas from the district sales office.

Reports vary between 180 and 190 cars being produced, but it is known that the majority were built in April, with another 10 or so leaving the line in May. All were coupes wearing Pace Car White (paint code C), with white seats and blue carpets (42) and optional backup lights (BL). All Checkered Flag cars were wearing their unique commemorative decal packages when accepted by the dealers, a fact verified by a photograph showing the assembled group. None were fitted with side mirrors, as those were generally installed by the dealerships on arrival. Each car came with an F-code, two-barrel 260-cid V-8 and automatic transmission. The first batch of 180 (five for each of 36 sales districts) featured sequential vehicle identification (VIN) numbers, although the district sales office (DSO) designations were different.

Indy 500 Mustangs from 1964-1/2 have such a low survival rate that some books mistakenly state Ford never built any replicas for sale to the public, but official company records and archived photos tell a different story.

All Mustang pace car replicas were powered by the 260-cid V-8 and an automatic transmission. *(Brad Bowling)*

No pace car replica delivered to "Checkered Flag" dealers received side mirrors, which were an option on regular Mustangs. *(Brad Bowling)*

Pace car replica stripes ran along the center of the hood, roof and decklid. *(Brad Bowling)*

Ford's early pictures of a pace car prototype show spinner hubcaps, but all production replica models were equipped with the standard cap. *(Brad Bowling)*

All pace car replicas had markings similar to these on their radiator supports at one time. On this car, they have been preserved. *(Brad Bowling)*

This ad promoted Ford's pace car duties for 1964. *(Don Hughmanick)*

All pace car replicas came with white seats, headliner and door panels and blue carpet. Ford's optional seatbelts were fitted to all pace cars. *(Brad Bowling)*

Unlike other 1964-1/2 Mustangs, each of the estimated 190 Indy pace car replicas came standard with backup lights. *(Brad Bowling)*

THE FACTS

Model Year	1964-1/2
How Many Were Made?	180-190
Engine	260-cid V-8
Reason for Limited Edition	commemorate Indy 500 pace duties
What Made It Special?	part of a dealer incentive contest, first special edition Mustang
Registries/Clubs	Indy Pace Car Registry of Mustangs PO Box 261251 Lakewood, CO 80226
Books	*Indy 500 Pace Cars* (1997, Auto Editors of *Consumer Guide*)

1964-1/2 Indy Pace Car Replica • 11

1979 Indy Pace Car Replica

photo cars owned by Monty Seawright and Daniel Carpenter

As has been its practice with the Mustang since inception, Ford promoted maximum production efficiency by building the third-generation model on the back of an existing platform. The "Fox" unit-body chassis had already been in passenger car service for a year as the Ford Fairmont and Mercury Zephyr when the 1979 Mustang debuted.

The entire domestic auto industry was just waking up to the benefits of aerodynamic design in the late 1970s, but Ford bypassed GM and Chrysler with the Mustang's slippery 0.44 coefficient of drag. Square frontal areas and tall, upright windshields caused an enormous amount of wind drag on the traditional American car, but shaping the Mustang more like a drop of water than a barn door made it more fuel efficient and a more comfortable experience for the driver.

The '79's construction from advanced plastics, aluminum, high-strength steel and thinner but stronger glass shaved 200 pounds from the Mustang's II's weight, bringing both hatchback and notchback in at around the 2,600-pound range.

Because of the overall weight loss in key areas, designers were free to add some needed inches to the new car's interior (which increased in volume by more than 20 percent) and exterior (length increased by four inches). Visibility was improved by a lowered glass line and gently sloped hood. Triangular rear quarter windows were critical components of the greenhouse as they offered a generous view to the sides of the car without opening. Recessed quad rectangular headlamps were installed for the first time on a Mustang in 1979. The grille had a crosshatch pattern and angled forward at the base.

The black band across the roof looks a lot like the "targa" strip on the 1978 King Cobra. Coincidence? *(Brad Bowling)*

Whether or not to apply the door decals was left up to the customer. *(Brad Bowling)*

Marchal foglamps sit recessed in the squared-off front airdam. *(Brad Bowling)*

Only a keen eye could spot the difference between this replica and the actual Indy pace car. *(Brad Bowling)*

Dual orange pinstripes ran the length of the pace car replica. (Brad Bowling)

This Indy replica came with the 5.0-liter V-8. (Brad Bowling)

Ford's advertising of the "European influenced" Mustang did not make note of the fact that engine options had not changed substantially since the Mustang II's introductory years. The 2.3-liter four-cylinder, 2.8-liter V-6, and 5.0-liter V-8 were essentially carryovers from 1978, but complementing the body of the future was an optional turbocharged version of the 2.3-liter rated at 131 horsepower. Ads promised "V-8 performance without sacrificing fuel economy" and a zero-to-55 time of just over eight seconds.

Innovations ran throughout the 1979 Mustang, including a single serpentine pulley belt, hydraulic shock strut, and four-bar link-and-coil rear suspension system.

The modern suspension could be enhanced with a basic handling package that included 14-inch radial tires with different spring rates and shock valving, stiffer bushings, and a special rear stabilizer bar. For Mustangers seeking greater road thrills, the Michelin TRX tire option featured ultra-low (for the time) aspect ratio tires that had first seen duty on Ford's European Granada. Because of the TRX's unusual size (15.35 inches in diameter, or 390mm), special metric alloy wheels were required.

All 1979 Mustangs had dashboards with full instruments, including tachometer, trip odometer, and gauges for fuel, oil pressure, alternator, and temperature. Interiors were also blessed with bucket seats, simulated woodgrain instrument panel appliqué, and stalk-mounted controls (to activate horn, headlamp dimmer and wiper/washer). Standard equipment for the chassis included rack-and-pinion steering, manual front disc brakes, and a front stabilizer bar. Also standard were vinyl door trim with carpeted lower panel, squeeze-open lockable glovebox, day/night mirror, lighter, black remote driver's mirror, and full wheel covers. Fastbacks had black rocker panel moldings, full wraparound body side moldings with dual accent stripe insert, and semi-styled wheels with black sport hub covers and trim rings. Quite a few options joined the list this year, including a sport-tuned exhaust, cruise control, tilt steering, leather seat trim, and interval windshield wipers.

Reaching back into the recent past, Ford built a Cobra package around its turbocharged engine (although the V-8 could be specified) and hatchback body. For an additional $1,173 over the price of a base Mustang, buyers received a special hood scoop, "Turbo" nameplate, the TRX handling components, blacked-out greenhouse trim, black lower bodyside tape treatment, and wraparound bodyside moldings with dual color-keyed inserts. Also included on the Cobra were color-keyed grille and quarter louvers, dual sport mirrors, black bumper rub strips with dual color-keyed inserts, an 8000-rpm tachometer, engine-turned instrument cluster panel, sport-tuned exhaust, and bright tailpipe extension. Rocker panel moldings were deleted on Cobras; optional hood graphics cost $78 extra.

The enduring third-generation Mustang icon, however, would be the three silver-and-black hatchbacks that paced the 63rd running of the Indianapolis 500 and the 10,478 replicas Ford produced and sold.

Jack Roush Performance Engineering built the three

A leather-wrapped steering wheel was standard with the Indy package, unless the customer ordered a tilt column. (Brad Bowling)

Though a little garish by today's standards, the orange and red striping visually lowered the body of the car. *(Brad Bowling)*

race-duty pace car engines from stock 302 blocks, to which the company added a Boss 302 crankshaft, high-performance connecting rods, TRW pistons, and a slew of vintage Ford go-fast parts. Early 351 Windsor heads, a dual-plane aluminum high-rise intake manifold, and a 600-cfm Holley four-barrel carburetor allowed for heavy breathing and boosted horsepower to an estimated 280. Each car received a three-speed C-4 automatic transmission modified for reliability and quicker shifts. The TRX handling suspension was lowered one inch for safety in handling the big oval's nearly flat corners, and Cars and Concepts custom installed the pace cars' T-roof panels.

Ford correctly predicted a huge demand for copies of the car Jackie Stewart drove during the Indy 500 parade lap. The replicas, built between April and July, wore the same special pewter and satin-black color scheme, blacked out trim, unique grille and deep front air dam, Marchal fog lights, a reverse-style hood scoop, Recaro bucket seats with a distinctive checkered pattern, leather-wrapped steering wheel, and simulated engine-turned dash inserts. Available options included air conditioning, tinted glass, tilt steering wheel (which canceled the leather-wrapped standard unit), four-way adjustable driver's seat, speed control, power door locks, rear window wiper/washer, and rear window defroster.

Orange and red striping flowed over the hood and along the sides of the replicas. Large decals reading "Official Pace Car" were shipped in each car to the dealer, as was the quite large front airdam (to avoid damage while loading and unloading). All replicas received the TRX handling suspension (minus the one-inch Indy drop) and all its upgraded springs, shocks, wheels, and tires.

Motivation was provided by either the Turbo Four or 5.0-liter. Of the 10,478 replicas built for the public, 5,970 were turbocharged, 2,402 had V-8s and four-speeds, and 2,106 had V-8s with automatic transmissions. The San Jose, Calif., plant produced 2,844 of the replicas; Dearborn pumped out 7,634.

Ford was serious about its pace car program, assigning a special VIN to each vehicle for authentication purposes. The sixth and seventh characters must be "48" for the Mustang to be an original pace car replica.

New base Mustang prices ranged from $4,071 to $5,097, with the pace car model listing for $9,012 before options. Ford projected sales of 330,000 Mustangs at the start of the 1979 model year, but exceeded expectations by producing 369,936, only 14.3 percent of which were equipped with 5.0-liter V-8s.

THE FACTS

Model Year	1979
How Many Were Made?	10,478
Engines	2.3-liter Turbo Four or 5.0-liter V-8
Reason for Limited Edition	commemorate Indy 500 pace duties
What Made It Special?	specific color, equipment level, graphics, turbo option
Registries/Clubs	Indy Pace Car Registry of Mustangs PO Box 261251 Lakewood, CO 80226 mustangpaceregistry.stangnet.com
Books	*Indy 500 Pace Cars* (1997, Auto Editors of *Consumer Guide*)

Indy Pace Car Replica 1994

photo car owned by Dennis Reardon

The 30th anniversary of the Mustang was met with corporate-sponsored enthusiasm and a range of fresh models from a basic V-6 coupe to a tire-burning Cobra convertible. Introduced on Oct. 15, 1993, as a 1994 model, the new Mustang was essentially a thorough, high-tech updating of the 1979 Fox chassis by a group of dedicated Ford employees known as "Team Mustang."

With a tight budget and tighter schedule, Team Mustang set up shop in an old Montgomery Ward warehouse near Dearborn late in 1990. Their aggressive goals were to meet high standards for ride, handling, steering, powertrain performance, brakes, climate control, comfort, and noise/vibration/harshness levels. The "SN-95" project (Ford-speak for sporty, North American market, concept 95) carried over approximately 520 Fox parts, but they were so buried in the chassis as to be invisible to the average enthusiast.

Chassis stiffness was a known weakness of the 1979-93 generation (especially when the unplanned convertible came along), so engineering goals for rigidity on the new platform were set quite high. The new convertible improved by 80 percent in the area of chassis torsion and 40 percent in bending, while the coupe (a hatchback body had been eliminated early in the planning process) saw upgrades of 44 percent in torsion and 56 percent in bending. Rigidity was increased through techniques such as bonding the windshield and backlight to their frames with a rigid urethane adhesive and by enlarging certain box sections such as the rocker panels and roof rails. Even the open-air convertible benefited from a thicker gauge of metal in the rocker panels (from 0.8 to 2.3 mm) as well as other stress-bearing panels. To ensure a quiet topless ride, a 25-pound tuned mass damper was installed inside the right front fender well.

New 17-inch wheels were fitted to all Cobras for 1994. *(Brad Bowling)*

The tan Saddle leather seats were marked with pace car insignia. *(Brad Bowling)*

Indy-specific decals were shipped with the car, but installed only at the buyer's request. *(Brad Bowling)*

The actual pace cars had automatic transmissions for safety considerations; replicas came with Borg-Warner's T-5 manual featuring phosphate-coated gears and stronger bearings. *(Brad Bowling)*

The aerodynamic 1994 Mustang body featured smooth, integrated headlights/parking signals; a smiling grille cavity; a long, sloping hood; and a dome-like top with a gentle radius. Every exterior dimension was greater for '94 when compared to the Fox body's '79 introduction: 181.5 inches bumper to bumper (2.4 inches longer); 101.3 inches hub to hub (.9 inches longer); 71.9 inches door handle to door handle (2.8 inches wider); and 52.9 inches floor to roof (1.4 inches higher). Tail lamps mimicked the original Mustang's three-element design, but in a horizontal layout.

Ford dropped the 2.3-liter four-cylinder option from the Mustang line, substituting the Taurus/Thunderbird/Continental's 3.8-liter 145-horsepower V-6 as standard for a 38% increase in power. A low-profile intake manifold and hypereutectic aluminum alloy pistons were the only major changes made to the GT's 5.0-liter V-8, which was rated at 215 horsepower. Both engines were available with standard five-speed manual or optional four-speed automatic transmissions.

Four-wheel disc brakes became standard equipment on all Mustangs for the first time in the marque's history, and Ford offered everything from a 15-inch steel wheel with plastic covers to 17-inchers and Goodyear Eagle GTs to hide them.

Convertibles had a power retractable soft top with a hard convertible top boot, illuminated visor mirrors, power deck lid release, power door locks and power side windows. The 1994 was Ford's first post-1973 Mustang convertible to be built as a topless car on the factory assembly line; earlier ragtops started life as coupes and had their roofs removed. A glass backlight was standard, with a built-in defroster costing extra. Convertible tops came in Black, White, or Saddle.

The Cobra's rear valance was shared with Ford's V-6 Mustangs. *(Brad Bowling)*

Sticker prices for the 1994 Mustang were reasonable for the time. The base coupe retailed for $13,355, the base convertible $20,150, the GT coupe $17,270, and the GT convertible $21,950.

One step above the GT on the performance ladder was SVT's Cobra, a continuation of the line introduced in 1993. Featuring a 240-horsepower version of the 5.0-liter V-8, the Cobra's taller intake manifold that required the use of a special hood for clearance as well as removal of the GT's strut tower-to-cowl stiffener brace. Model-unique engine compartment touches included a "Cobra"-stamped plenum plate, special valve covers, an accessory belt and lower radiator hose stamped with the car's model name, and a standard engine oil cooler.

SVT engineers set the Cobra's suspension to softer specs than what the GT used, with the front linear-rate units rated at 400 pounds per square inch and rears handling 160. Likewise, smaller diameter sway bars (25mm in front, 27mm in back) contributed to passenger comfort.

All 1,000 1994 SVT Cobra convertibles were Rio Red pace car replicas. *(Brad Bowling)*

Visually, the Cobra differed from the GT by virtue of its front bumper fascia incorporating perfectly round foglamps (the GT's were smaller and rectangular), crystal clear, European-style reflector headlamps and an LED brake light embedded in the rear spoiler. Emblems depicting coiled snakes replaced the GT fender badges, even though a galloping pony still took center stage in the grille opening. The Cobra's rear valance panel, lifted from Ford's V-6 model, read "Mustang." Exterior colors were limited for 1994 to Rio Red, Crystal White, and Black.

The "Cobra" name was embossed on the steering wheel, and model-unique floor mats, white-faced gauges (including a 160-mph speedometer), and leather-wrapped shift knob were standard equipment.

Brakes were Bosch three-channel ABS-assisted and measured 13.0 inches in front with twin-piston "Cobra" calipers; rears were vented and measured 11.65 inches in diameter. Tire sizes increased from 1993, with SVT installing 255/45ZR-17 uni-directional Eagle GS-Cs on five-spoke, 17x8-inch alloy rims, and a 17-inch mini spare was tucked away in the trunk.

On May 29, 1994, a trio of Cobra convertibles served as pace cars for the 78th installment of the Indianapolis 500, all slightly modified for heavy-duty pacing. The race-day pace cars were modified at Jack Roush's shop in Allen Park, Mich., with heavy-duty four-speed automatic transmissions, 15-gallon racing fuel cells, heavier rear springs (to accommodate the weight of television camera equipment), a Halon fire-extinguisher system, a rollbar with 50,000-watt strobe lights built in and special lights in the rear spoiler. Parnelli Jones, a seven-time Indy competitor whose single win took place in 1963, drove the official pace car; Al Unser Jr. won the race, his second Indy 500 victory.

The Cobra's 5.0-liter V-8 was rated at 240 horsepower, which was certainly adequate for pace car duty. *(Brad Bowling)*

To commemorate the occasion, SVT produced 1,000 Rio Red replicas with Saddle leather interiors and Saddle tops at $26,845 each. As with most pace car knock-offs, decals were shipped to the dealers inside the cars (not on them) and left to the buyer's discretion to install. SVT also sold 5,009 Cobra coupes at $20,765 apiece.

It should be noted that Ford built 107 "festival" Mustang convertibles with full decal packages for use by Indianapolis Motor Speedway staff and celebrities during the event, but they were Rio Red GTs—not Cobras—with Saddle leather interiors and automatic transmissions. All 107 were returned to Ford and sold to the public after the race.

THE FACTS

Model Year	1994
How Many Were Made?	1,000
Engine	240-horsepower 5.0-liter V-8
Reason for Limited Edition	to commemorate Indy 500 pace duties
What Made It Special?	specific color, equipment level, graphics
Registries/Clubs	Indy Pace Car Registry of Mustangs PO Box 261251 Lakewood, CO 80226
Books	*Indy 500 Pace Cars* (1997, Auto Editors of *Consumer Guide*) *SVT Mustang Cobra Recognition Guide: 1993-2000* (1999, Thomas A Shreiner & Peter C. Sessler)

1994 Indy Pace Car Replica • 17

SECTION 2:

National Promotions

Don't be fooled by the pretty face! The Mustang's sex appeal, sporty personality, and long option list were certainly motivating factors behind the car's initial success, but Ford's total commitment to the product in terms of advertising and coordinating its sales force are what kept the pony running at the front of the herd for many years.

The first wave of Mustang fever and unprecedented buyer enthusiasm took Ford and the world by surprise, but the company quickly recovered its composure and developed a series of national promotions to ensure foot traffic in its dealerships.

In the 1960s, springtime was considered the prime opportunity for car companies to beef up sales. People were recovered from Christmas spending, would be traveling during the summer months, and had been looking at the same "new" cars for six months already.

Considering the Mustang itself was introduced in April, it's clear that nobody played the spring sales game like Ford Motor Company. Less than two years after its debut, Ford was ready to sell Mustang number 1,000,000! That is an astounding figure since many car models have come and gone without selling a million copies over an entire decade. To publicize its success—and further build on it—in 1966 Ford issued the first of an informal series of national promotions aimed at getting budget-minded buyers to look at the Mustang. The "Sprint" cars were the mainstay of Ford's spring promotions throughout much of the 1960s and into the early '70s, and brought a high perceived value to base Mustang models at no extra cost.

Should the 1966-68 and '72 Sprints be considered separate Mustang models, or just cosmetic packages? From a technical standpoint, the Sprints were simply packages applied to existing models—for most years the VIN and data plate give no indication of special status—but history gives them an importance that is hard to overlook.

Today, car company sales pushes have evolved into incentive wars and rebate battles, which will not be nearly as interesting to study as chrome air cleaners and wire wheel hubcaps.

Cars Not Found in this Chapter

Ford had planned a **Bandito** model for 1969, but there is not enough information available to suggest it was ever produced. By strange coincidence the Frito-Lay potato chip company canceled its popular "Frito Bandito" mascot in '69 after complaints from the Mexican Anti-Defamation Committee. Perhaps seeing the cartoon Bandito get Frito Lay-ed off made Ford reconsider its limited-edition of the same name.

1966-68 Sprints

photo car owned by Dennis Degnor ('66 Sprint)
photo car owned by Brian Wingard ('67 Sports Sprint)
photo car owned by Jim Gillespie ('68 Sprint)

In 1966 Ford still had the pony car market all to itself, but the company knew its Mustang monopoly would end in '67 with the introduction of competition from GM, Chrysler, and even AMC. To stoke the public's buying frenzy, Ford poured truckloads of dollars into creative and funny advertisements that boasted of the sale of its millionth Mustang, the Walter Mitty-like fantasy of owning such a car and the "Six" appeal of its base model.

The ads did not, however, play up the $44 price increase for the hardtop. The fastback and convertible also experienced sticker jump, with $18 and $49 respectively being added for '66.

This '66 Sprint has the dealer-installed air conditioning system. *(Jerry Heasley)*

Unwilling to mess with success, Ford made only minor cosmetic changes to the '66, such as a revised instrument panel (that looked less like the Falcon it came from), more ornate trim on the car's side, and a different grille design. Other improvements to the Mustang were federally mandated: front and rear seat belts, padded instrument panel, emergency flashers, electric wipers, and windshield washers as standard equipment.

The list of regular Mustang features included front bucket seats, pleated vinyl upholstery and interior trim, Sports-type steering wheel, five-dial instrument cluster, full carpeting, heater and defroster, left-hand door outside rearview mirror, back-up lamps, door courtesy lights, rocker panel moldings, full wheel covers, three-speed manual transmission with floor lever control, and 200-cid 120-hp six-cylinder engine. The fastback also came with special Silent-Flo ventilation, and the base V-8 was the 200-hp version of the 289-cid engine.

For its traditional spring sales promotion in 1966, Ford created a simple but elegant feature package for the Mustang known popularly as the

With only 6,000 miles on the odometer, this '66 Sprint displays all-original components, such as the chrome air cleaner housing. *(Jerry Heasley)*

Don't be fooled by the standard '66 hubcaps on this Sprint coupe. The Sprint's original wire wheels were shipped in the cars' trunks to avoid damage during shipping. It is most likely the case that this concours Sprint had its wires pilfered by the selling dealer before the car was delivered. *(Jerry Heasley)*

"Sprint 200." Based on the 200-cid six-cylinder base engine (T code), the Sprint was available in any color, body style, and equipment level, but it came standard with a chrome air cleaner (wearing a special Sprint 200 decal), center console, body side accent pinstripes, and wire wheel hubcaps at no extra cost.

The six-cylinder was highlighted for two reasons: 1) Ford was experiencing a shortage of its popular V-8s, and 2) the Sprint 200 was seen as a great attraction for thousands of budget-minded Mustang lovers. Although ads describing the Sprint package declared April to be "Millionth Mustang Month," it was available most of the selling season. Most advertisements made no mention of a "Sprint"—the package was simply referred to as a "specially priced, specially equipped model."

Ford lost or destroyed nearly all of its 1965-66 production records, so there is no accurate indication of how successful the Sprint promotion was. Registries and unscientific car show observations suggest most Sprint 200s were hardtops and that the more expensive convertible was ordered much less frequently. The fastback body style is perhaps the rarest of all 1966 Sprint 200s. Unlike many special edition Mustangs, Sprints were not produced at one plant in a batch; all three Mustang factories built them as ordered throughout much of the year.

Unlike the 1966 model year, Sprints ordered in '67 could be had with six-cylinder or V-8 power. *(Jerry Heasley)*

It is nearly impossible to authenticate a '66 Sprint because there was no indicator in the VIN, data plate, or build sheets. Historians must rely on old-fashioned word-of-mouth techniques and the original paper trail to verify suspected Sprints.

By 1967, Ford's Mustang sales advantage versus the new Chevrolet Camaro, Pontiac Firebird, and Mercury Cougar was shrinking, but giving the original pony car a jazzy new body, wider track for better road grip, a broader range of engines, and a longer options list kept it ahead of the pack.

The re-design was nothing radical. The '67 model strongly resembled the '65 America had fallen in love

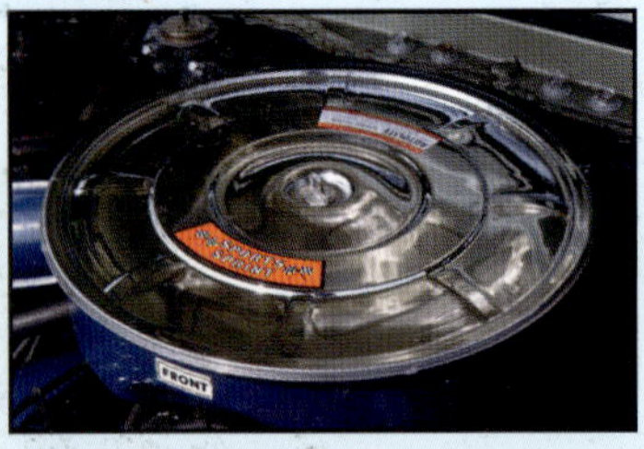

The tradition of a chrome air cleaner cover on Sprints started in 1966 and continued into '67. *(Jerry Heasley)*

1967 Sprint buyers received a discount on Ford's factory-installed air-conditioning system. *(Jerry Heasley)*

Ford sold more Sports Sprint packages in 1967 than some manufacturers sold cars. *(Jerry Heasley)*

The '68 Sprint model was available with six-cylinder or V-8 power. *(Don Hughmanick)*

Ford ads promoting the '68 Sprint stressed the low price. *(Don Hughmanick)*

with, but everything was just a bit larger. Its grille formed a more pronounced opening; side feature lines led to a bigger simulated air scoop; taillights formed three vertical lenses on each side of a concave indentation panel; and the centrally located gas cap had a new look. Overall length, tread, and width grew, but the wheelbase stayed the same. Designers made the 2+2 roofline more dramatic by pulling it all the way to the rear of the decklid.

Mustang engine compartments could be stuffed with big-block power for the first time in 1967. For only $264, a buyer could take home an S-code 390-cid/320-hp powerplant with plenty of neck-snapping street performance and some dragstrip bragging rights.

All other '67 Mustang engines were carryovers from the previous year. A one-year-only designation made GTs with automatic transmissions into GTAs.

Having enjoyed much success with its 1966 Sprint package, Ford expanded the idea in the spring of '67 to

The 1968 Sprint was available in six-cylinder or V-8 form. This photo car has optional dealer-installed landau bars. *(Jerry Heasley)*

From this angle the Sprint's pop-up gas cap and GT stripe are visible. *(Jerry Heasley)*

1966-68 Sprints • 21

create the Sports Sprint. Standard Sprint features included a louvered hood with integrated turn signal indicators, whitewall tires, full wheel covers, bright rocker panel moldings, a chrome air cleaner, and a vinyl-covered shift lever if ordered with the SelectShift Cruise-O-Matic transmission. The 200-cid six-cylinder was considered the base engine, but buyers could upgrade to a 289-cid V-8 with two-barrel carburetor (C code). Sports Sprints were only available in coupe or convertible body styles. The package also included a special price on factory-installed SelectAire air conditioning.

As before, all three factories turned out Sprints for most of the production year, and there are no clear identifiers in the VIN, warranty plate, or build sheet. According to Kevin Marti's *Mustang...by the Numbers (1967-1973)*, Ford sold 109,946 Sports Sprint packages in 1967—101,419 as hardtops, 8,527 as convertibles—but there is no breakout between the six-cylinder and V-8 engines.

The 1968 Mustang was not substantially different from the '67 version, but that doesn't mean there was no excitement in the air! A midyear offering, the R-code 428-cid/335-horsepower Cobra Jet big-block V-8, turned the sporty pony car into a dragstrip terror! Mustang buyers could also specify one of two new 302-cid V-8s: a 220-horsepower two-barrel version (code F) or a 230-horse four-barrel powerplant (J). Returning from '67 was the 390-cid/325-horsepower S-code big-block V-8. The 200-cid six-cylinder and 289-cid V-8 with two-barrel carburetor remained base engines.

Cosmetic modifications for 1968 included a front end with the Mustang emblem "floating" in the grille; script-style (instead of block letters) Mustang body side nameplates; and cleaner-looking bright metal trim on the cove (replacing the previous "cheese graters"). There was a new two-tone hood that predicted the more radical coloring to come on the 1969 Mach 1s and Bosses. Despite minimal changes in the product, prices rose substantially, averaging about $140 more per model.

A sportier look could be had by ordering the $147 GT option, which brought with it a choice of stripes (the reflective "C" or rocker panel type), auxiliary lights in the grille, a GT gas cap, and GT wheelcovers. On the 1968 Mustang, the extra lights no longer had a bar separating them from the corral in the grille. Front disc brakes were usually extra-cost, but were standard when big-block V-8s were ordered. A total of 17,458 GTs were made in 1968.

There were two Sprint packages offered for 1968 as part of Ford's "See the Light" sale. Package A, which was available with six-cylinder and V-8 engines, included GT stripes, a pop-open gas cap, and full wheel covers. Package B, which could only be had with V-8 power, brought GT stripes, a pop-open gas cap, Wide Oval tires, styled-steel wheels, and GT foglamps.

According to Marti, Ford sold 25,012 1968 Sprint coupes with Package A (plus one fastback and one convertible) and 15,105 coupes with Package B (plus one fastback).

THE FACTS

Model Year	1966-68
How Many Were Made?	n/a (1966)
	101,419 (1967)
	40,117 (1968)
Engines	200-cid I-6, 289/2V V-8
Reason for Limited Edition	boost Mustang sales in spring
What Made It Special?	luxury features at no extra cost
Registries/Clubs	1966 Spring 200 Registry/Early Six
	27534 140th Ave. SE
	Kent, WA 98042
Books	*Mustang Recognition Guide* (1981, Larry Dobbs, Donald Farr, Jerry Heasley, and Rick Kopec)
	25 Years of Mustang Advertising (1989, Jerry Heasley)

Special Value Package 1971

For 1971 Ford blew up its Mustangs to gargantuan proportions, making them the lowest, widest, longest, and heaviest models to ever sport the running horse emblem. Built around the winning long hood/short trunk profile of the original, the cars looked more like muscular distant cousins to the 1964-1/2 Mustang that had won America's hearts.

Some new features were apparent at a glance—the full-width grille that incorporated round headlights, a flatter roof shape, a "tunnel backlite" (recessed rear window) on every hardtop coupe and nearly horizontal pane of glass at the rear of each fastback.

Bigger in every way than their predecessors, the 1971 Mustangs had a slightly longer wheelbase than the '70 models (109 vs. 108 inches) and were 2.1 inches longer overall at 189.5 (7.1 inches more than the original. Width increased by 3.0 inches over the '70 model and 6.8 inches beyond the 1964-1/2. All of that extra sheetmetal added 500 pounds to the 1971's weight—that's family sedan territory today!

Ford's desire to make the Mustang a car for all purses and purposes had it evolving into a platform suitable for a supercar or luxurious and spacious daily transportation for a sporty young family. Big-block Mustang power had been available since the 390-cid S-code V-8 was introduced in '67, but usually with great compromise. The Boss 429, for example, had required an outside company and a big shoehorn to mate the wide big-block to the '69 Mustang, which product planners saw as a weak point in the car's design. They sought to fix the situation with an engine compartment big enough to handle any powerplant in the Ford family.

Unfortunately for all the young families in need of 400-horsepower grocery getters, Ford's timing and instincts were off slightly. During the 1968-70 period when the '71 was being developed, car companies and the American buyer were willing partners in a horsepower escalation that seemed to have no end. Just as the giant new Mustangs were introduced, the government and insurance companies put the brakes on all that enthusiasm, leading a lot of longtime Ford customers to ask, "why so big?"

Sales were slow, but it wasn't from a lack of sporty product or sales effort. The fastback body style was now called the "SportsRoof." The coupe-only Grandé and SportsRoof-based Mach 1 and Boss models were back; however, a new 331-horsepower 351-cid V-8 (code R) Cleveland engine replaced the previous year's Boss 302 and 429 powerplants.

Bumpers and fender and hood moldings were chrome plated, except on Mach 1s and Boss 351s. The corral around the chrome pony returned to the center of the grille on standard models, but an optional grille deleted the corral while offering amber auxiliary lights in the honeycomb-textured surface. With the sport grille came a small tri-bar emblem.

Standard equipment for Mustangs included color-keyed nylon carpeting; floor-mounted shift lever; high-back bucket seats; steel door guard rails; DirectAire ventilation; concealed wipers with cowl air inlets; a mini-console with ash tray; arm rests; courtesy lights; a cigar lighter; a heater and defroster; an all-vinyl interior; a glove box; the 250-cid six; E78-14 fiberglass-belted, black sidewall tires; and, on convertibles, a power top.

To that list the coupe-only Grandé added bright pedal pad surrounds; deluxe cloth high-back bucket seat trim; deluxe instrument panel trim; a deluxe, two-spoke steering wheel; an electric clock; molded trim panels with integral pull handles and arm rests; a rear ash tray in the right quarter trim panel; dual accent paint stripes; color-keyed dual racing mirrors (left-hand mirror remote-controlled); rocker panel moldings; vinyl roof; full wheelcovers; and wheel lip moldings.

Mach 1s came standard with the basic SportsRoof equipment, plus a color-keyed spoiler/bumper with color-keyed hood and front fender moldings. Also color-keyed were the dual racing mirrors, with the left-hand mirror featuring remote-control operation. Mach 1s came standard

The 1971 Special Value Package is often referred to as the "Sport Coupe." (Don Hughmanick)

with the sport lamp grille; competition suspension; hubcaps and trim rings; a black, honeycomb-textured back panel appliqué; a pop-open gas cap; a deck lid paint stripe; black or argent silver lower body side finish with bright moldings at the upper edge; E70-14 whitewalls; and the base V-8. NASA-style hood scoops were optional at no extra charge.

For only the second time in its history the Mustang's base engine increased in size, although the L-code 250-cid/145-horsepower inline six-cylinder with single-barrel carburetor struggled to move the big 1971 model. Standard V-8 for the line was the F-code 210-hp/302-cid with two-barrel carburetor; a few dollars more bought the 351-cid/240-horse H-code or 351-cid/285-horse M-code powerplants.

The two truly exciting speed options for 1971 were the Boss 351 (R code) and 429 Cobra Jet (C code) performance packages. Similar in looks to the Mach 1, the Boss' standard equipment included all of the Mustang basics, plus a functional NASA-style hood with Black or Argent Silver full hood paint treatment, hood lock pins, and Ram Air engine decals. Also featured were racing mirrors; honeycombed grille; hubcaps and trim rings; black or argent silver body side tape stripes (these also became optional on Mach 1s late in the year); color-keyed hood and front fender moldings; Boss 351 nomenclature; dual exhausts; power front disc brakes; a Space-Saver spare tire; a competition suspension with staggered rear shocks; a 3.91:1 axle ratio with Traction-Lok differential; a functional black spoiler, shipped "knocked-down" inside the car for dealer installation; an 80-ampere battery; Ford's Instrumentation Group option; an electronic rpm-limiter; high-back bucket seats; a special cooling package; a wide-ratio four-speed manual transmission with Hurst shifter; the 351-cid H.O. (high-output) V-8 with 330 hp; and F60-15 belted blackwall tires. A chrome bumper was standard on Boss 351s, while the Mach 1-style color-keyed bumper was an option.

Contrary to legend the big-block Mustangs have generated, the 429 V-8 available in 1971 was in no way related to the Boss powerplant of 1969-70, which was derived from Ford's "semi-hemi" NASCAR racing engine. They were actually 460-cid blocks from Thunderbirds and Lincolns destroked to 429 cubic inches and topped with "wedge" heads.

The new 429 Cobra Jet (429CJ) engine sold for $372 more than the cost of the base V-8, and could be installed in any Mustang body style. A 429 Cobra Jet Ram Air (429CJ-R) option was $436 above the base V-8. Both were rated at 370 hp. A 429 Super Cobra Jet with Dual Ram Air induction and a 375-hp rating was available for $531 over the base V-8. Hydraulic valve lifters, four-bolt main caps, dress-up aluminum valve covers and a GM Quadrajet four-barrel carburetor were part of the 429CJ-R performance package. The 429SCJ-R featured mechanical lifters, adjustable rocker arms, a larger Holley four-barrel carburetor, and forged pistons.

Realizing its budget Mustang buyers would not pony up for Boss or Cobra Jet power, Ford created a cosmetic package to dress up the base coupe for springtime. Ads refer to it by the unexciting description "Special Spring Value," but Mustang enthusiasts consider it a continuation of the Springtime Sprint series. Looking for all the world like a hardtop Mach 1, the '71 Sprint featured the NASA-scooped hood, dual racing mirrors, color-keyed bumpers, Boss side stripes, and wide tires with Mach 1-style trim rings and hubcaps.

Information on the Sprint is scarce, but it is known that 9,003 packages were sold in a year that saw the once-popular Mach 1 drop to 36,498 units and overall Mustang production reach a new low of 149,678.

THE FACTS

Model Year	1971
How Many Were Made?	9,003
Engines	any available Mustang engine
Reason for Limited Edition	spring sales promotion
What Made It Special?	Boss-like graphics, NASA-scooped hood
Books	*25 Years of Mustang Advertising* (1989, Jerry Heasley) *Mustang...by the Numbers (1967-1973)* (2000, Kevin Marti)

1972 Sprint

photo car owned by Ben Mandell

Ford made no obvious visual changes to its popular Mustang for 1972, having introduced its bigger-than-ever body the year before. Although described in advertising as a "sports compact" model, the enlarged 1971-73 Mustang was comparable to today's full-size Taurus or Ford Five Hundred in terms of size and weight.

Powertrain choices were also carryovers in 1972, with a few glaring exceptions at the top of the performance ladder. Base models were equipped with a 250-cid inline six-cylinder rated at 98 horsepower, and V-8 alternatives were limited to a 136-horsepower 302/two-barrel, a 168-horse two-barrel 351, a 200-horsepower four-barrel 351, and a high-output 351 four-barrel engine with 275 ponies. All of Ford's engines were rated on an SAE net scale for 1972, which made them look on paper to be weaker than the '71 offerings, but they were identical. The standard transmission on a base Mustang was the three-speed manual, with a four-speed stick or three-speed automatic available at extra cost.

Three body styles broke down to five distinct models—hardtop, SportsRoof, convertible, Grandé, and Mach 1—all of which could be ordered with a variety of options and features. With the death of the high-performance Boss 351 fastback and powerful 429 Cobra Jet engine the previous year, Ford was hard pressed to sell its unchanged '72 Mustang as a musclecar so the company developed several appearance and cosmetic packages to lure customers.

Following a tradition established with the slow-selling 1966 six-cylinder Mustang, Ford developed a Sprint graphics and features package for the '72 model to share with its Maverick and Pinto stablemates. Corporate designers were told to make the new Sprint a real standout—something more than just a unique stripe or chrome air cleaner. What went on sale in the spring of '72

Unlike the 1966 version, which was only available with the 200-cid six-cylinder, 1972 Sprints could be ordered with a variety of engines. *(Brad Bowling)*

The Sprint's USA shield was flying proudly in an Olympic year. *(Brad Bowling)*

This 1972 Mustang convertible with Sprint dress package is one of 50 droptops built for a special event. *(Brad Bowling)*

This bulletin was sent to Ford dealers as part of their regular marketing updates. In '72, it prepared the sales force for the upcoming Sprint models. *(Don Hughmanick)*

Dealer information discussed the '72 Mustang Sprints as being hardtops and fastbacks only. *(Don Hughmanick)*

As is often the case, the Mustang was promoted as a lifestyle enhancement in this '72 Sprint ad. *(Don Hughmanick)*

was one of the most attractive and eye-catching limited-edition packages ever available from Ford.

Ford unofficially glommed onto the patriotic fervor that developed in America at the beginning of the Olympic year by offering to the public its Mustang hardtop and SportsRoof in a special red-white-and-blue paint scheme. Sprint Package A was simply known as the Sprint Decor option. The bulk of the Mustang Sprint body was White (code 9A) with a light medium-blue tape appliqué around the lower perimeter. Two wide blue tape stripes decorated the hood. The tail lamp panel and rear valance were painted blue. A red pinstripe ran along the lower body, emphasizing the color break, as well as outlining the hood stripes. The interior was also two-tone white and blue. Each Sprint included dual white racing mirrors, color-keyed seats and carpets, and white sidewall tires with color-keyed hubcaps and trim rings. The rear fender wore an Olympic-style USA shield decal. Sprints had E70-14 whitewall tires on stamped steel wheels wearing color-keyed hubcaps and trim rings. The "B" Sprint package substituted Magnum 500 wheels, F60-15 raised white-letter tires, and a competition suspension.

Although Ford dealers were limited to fastbacks and hardtops when ordering the Sprint Decor option, it has been documented that 50 Sprint convertibles were built to transport beauty queens from every state in the Washington, D.C., Cherry Blossom Festival parade. (The festival celebrates a 1912 gift from the mayor of Tokyo to Washington: thousands of cherry trees that blossom every spring.) All 50 convertibles, which were equipped with the 302-cid two-barrel V-8 engines and automatic transmissions, rode the Dearborn assembly line in a single group and feature consecutive serial numbers.

According to Kevin Marti of Marti Autoworks (www.martiauto.com), 7,470 Sprints were ordered with the $156 A Package; 1,913 were built with the $347.46 B Package; 6,247 were hardtops; and 3,086 were fastbacks. The

The blue tail panel was standard on all Sprints, whether convertible, hardtop, or fastback. *(Brad Bowling)*

There was no optional interior color scheme for the '72 Sprint. *(Brad Bowling)*

26 • *Mustang Special Editions*

The Sprint package included these Lambeth cloth inserts in the door panels. *(Brad Bowling)*

For obvious reasons, very few of the Pinto and Maverick Sprints have survived. *(Don Hughmanick)*

Because it is lacking Magnum 500 wheels, this convertible was built with Sprint Package A. *(Brad Bowling)*

most popular engine choice was the 302 (5,624 ordered), followed by the two-barrel 351 (2,957), 250-cid six (414), and four-barrel 351 (388).

It has been suggested that Ford sold a similar package through its Canadian dealers in 1972, but with a maple leaf decal instead of the USA shield. There is currently no documentation to support this claim.

Although it was a sales and public relations success, the 1972 Sprint campaign would be Ford's last as of this printing.

THE FACTS

Model Year	1972
How Many Were Made?	9,383
Engines	250/1V I-6, 302/2V V-8, 351/2V V-8, or 351/4V V-8
Reason for Limited Edition	continuation of spring sales promotion, an unofficial nod to that year's Olympic games
What Made It Special?	visual effect, paint, equipment level
Registries/Clubs	http://webpages.uah.edu/~russell
Books	*Mustang...By the Numbers (1967-1973)* (2000, Kevin Marti)

1995 GTS

The 30th anniversary of the Mustang, 1994, brought with it a new shape for the much-loved American icon. More than just a facelift, the new Mustang was essentially a high-tech updating of the '79 Fox chassis, which is why Ford referred to it as the "Fox-4" platform. Springing from the fertile minds and busy hands of "Team Mustang" (a group of Ford employees dedicated to the '94's concept and design), the smooth pony was made of 1,330 new parts and 520 carryovers from '93, including much of the powertrain.

Team Mustang's efforts to increase chassis stiffness over the '93 Fox package were rewarded with a 44 percent improvement for the coupe and 80 percent for the convertible. Numerous clever techniques made these goals possible, including bonding the windshield and backlight to their frames with a rigid urethane adhesive and enlarging certain box sections such as rocker panels and roof rails. Digging into the innovative Mustang aftermarket for ideas, Team Mustang installed a bolt-in brace to tie the front struts and firewall together to eliminate torque flex. Convertibles received a 25-pound tuned mass damper in the right front fender well.

To produce the Mustang line on a tighter budget, Ford reduced the number of choices for buyers to two body styles, two engines, two transmissions, and a handful of colors.

Ford killed off the once-popular hatchback by designing the new coupe with a fastback slope, thus reducing the number of 1994 body styles to two. The market goal for the Mustang's new look was that it would thrill some, appeal to others, but offend no one. Short, wide aerodynamic headlights sat on either side of a curved grille cavity that provided a pleasant, smiling face when combined with the smooth bumper cover and integrated air dam. To keep the Mustang's look traditional despite having a body tuned in the wind tunnel, designers stuck with the long hood/short deck proportions and sloped the air-cheating hood to suggest an extremely large engine. A gently radiused roof complemented the rounder body with its futuristic dome-like silhouette.

Although it looked compact, the '94 Mustang was 2.4 inches longer (181.5 inches bumper to bumper) than the '79 version, with a wheelbase increase of 0.9 inches (101.3 total). Girth increased as well, from 69.1 to 71.9 inches, and the roofline stood 1.4 inches higher at 52.9 inches.

Ford dropped the 2.3-liter four-cylinder engine from the line in 1994, switching to a 145-horsepower 3.8-liter V-6 (code 4, first used in Ford's Taurus and Thunderbird and Lincoln's Continental). This simple move increased the base model's horsepower by 38 percent. Hardcore Mustangers, though, were more interested in the GT's 215-horsepower 5.0-liter HO V-8 (E code), a virtual carryover from '93 but with 10 extra horses. Both powerplants came standard with a five-speed manual transmission; a four-speed automatic overdrive was available at extra cost with either choice.

Base V-6 cars—whether coupe or convertible—came with 15-inch steel wheels hiding behind plastic covers and wearing 205/65-15 all-season black sidewall Goodyear Eagle GA tires or, for a bit more money, three-spoke alloy rims could be ordered. GT standard wheels were five-spoke 16-inchers with 225/55-16 Firestone Firehawk doughnuts, but there was an extra-cost option of three-spoke 17-inch rims with 245/45-17 Goodyear Eagle GTs. For the first time in Mustang history, disc brakes came standard at all four corners, and ABS was an extra-cost option.

Base coupes ran $13,355 and convertibles stickered for $20,150. The standard equipment list was quite involved and well considered. It included front and rear body-colored fascias with Mustang nomenclature; Mustang emblem fender badges; aerodynamic halogen headlamps; wraparound tail lamps featuring three horizontal elements; dual, electric, remote-control mirrors (convex mirror on right-hand side); color-keyed rocker panel moldings; driver and passenger air bags; a front ashtray; three-point "active" seat belts; 16-ounce carpeting; a cigarette lighter; a digital quartz clock; a stand-alone console with armrest, storage bin, cup-holder and CD/cassette storage; a driver's side foot rest; a glove box; full-instrumentation (including tachometer and low-fluid lamp); an extensive Light Group assortment; dual visor mirrors with covers; reclining cloth bucket seats with cloth head restraints and four-way power driver's seat; split-back fold-down rear seat (not in convertibles); leather-wrapped shift knob and parking brake lever with automatic transmission; stalk-mounted controls; tilt steering with center horn-blow; soft, flow-through vinyl door trim panels with full armrests and cloth or vinyl inserts; a color-keyed headliner (including convertibles); color-keyed cloth sun visors; heavy-duty electrical components; power, side window de-misters; electronic engine control (EEC-V) system; stainless steel exhaust system; 15.4-gallon fuel tank with tethered cap; full tinted glass; Power Vent ventilation system; dual-note horn; a Power Lock Group option; a tunnel-mounted parking brake; an ETR stereo sound system with four 24-watt speakers; constant-ratio, power rack-and-pinion steering; modified MacPherson front suspension with stabilizer bar, links and coil springs; gas-pressurized front struts and rear shock absorbers; a mini-spare and interval-type windshield wipers.

Convertible buyers received a power retractable soft top with a folding hard boot, illuminated visor mirrors, power deck lid release, power door locks, and power side windows. The 1994 was Ford's first post-1973 Mustang convertible to be built as a topless car on the factory assembly line; earlier ragtops started life as coupes and had their roofs removed. A glass backlite was standard, with a built-in defroster costing extra. Convertible tops came in Black, White, or Saddle.

Ford offered 11 choices of eye-catching colors on the '94 Mustang, including Canary Yellow (GT only), Vibrant Red (GT only), Rio Red, Laser Red, Iris, Bright Blue, Deep Forest Green, Teal, Black, Opal Frost, and Crystal White. Interiors were available in five colors: Bright Red, Saddle, Opal Grey, Black, and White (convertible only).

The $17,270 GT coupe and $21,960 GT convertible included (or replaced) all of the standard equipment and added front and rear fascias with GT nomenclature and black finish on the lower rear end; Mustang GT fender badges; fog lamps; a single-wing rear spoiler; 16x7.5-inch wide five-spoke cast aluminum wheels with locks; a 150-mph speedometer; GT bucket seats with cloth trim, cloth head restraints, adjustable cushions, power lumbar support, and a four-way power driver's seat; a leather-wrapped steering wheel; a Traction-Lok rear axle; handling brace to stiffen the engine compartment ("similar to those utilized by Ford NASCAR teams," said the brochure); stainless steel dual exhaust system; GT suspension package with variable-rate coil springs, unique-calibrated gas struts and shocks, and Quadra-shock rear suspension with strut lever brace and illuminated visor mirrors with hard covers.

One of the most popular new options was the Mach 460 system that used eight speakers to put out 460 peak watts of sound. Ford sold 123,198 of its new Mustangs in 1994.

A rare guarantee in life is that any Mustang design in its second year will be significantly unchanged from its introductory season, which explains why the 1995 received only minor improvements. Prices increased slightly across the board for the base coupe ($14,330), base convertible ($20,795), GT coupe ($17,905), and GT convertible ($22,595).

Having won back the Mustang faithful with its renewed devotion to stylish, high-performance models, Ford acknowledged the final days of its legendary 5.0-liter V-8 by creating the budget-racer GTS package. Depending on where you stand on the whole "glass half empty, glass half full" perspective, the GTS coupe was either a GT stripped of all non-essential GT parts or a base model upgraded with the 5.0-liter engine and driveline. There were no sport seats, rear spoiler or foglamps on the $16,910 GTS, but it did include the GT's standard 16-inch five-spoke alloy rims. Manual locks and windows were standard, and any V-6 options could be added to the GTS.

There were no "GTS" badges made up for this economy musclecar; instead, the rear bumper cover declared "Mustang GT," and there were "GT" callouts on the fenders. Cloth seats were standard, as were air conditioning and an AM/FM stereo cassette player. The instrument cluster, with its 7000-rpm tach, 150-mph speedometer and other gauges, was borrowed from the GT.

Of the 6,370 GTS Mustangs built in 1995, 4,848 were fitted with five-speed transmissions and 1,522 had automatics. In fitting with its "sleeper" theme, most GTSs were ordered in Black (UA).

Sales greatly improved in the second year of the new Mustang design, with a total of 185,986 units sold—137,722 of which were coupes, and 48,264 of which were convertibles.

THE FACTS

Model Year	1995
How Many Were Made?	6,370
Engine	5.0-liter V-8
Reason for Limited Edition	final year for 5.0-liter
What Made It Special?	lighter, cheaper, equipment delete
Registries/Clubs	www.hillie16.stangnet.com

SECTION 3:
Regional Promotions

It is rare to walk into a Ford dealer today and find a special edition Mustang available only to that state or region, but such promotions were common in the 1960s and early '70s.

Just how "special" the edition was depended on the resourcefulness and creativity of the area dealers and the amount of pull they had with Ford Motor Company. Some specials, like the Indy Pacesetter, boasted nothing more than a unique decal. In other cases, such as with the California Special/High Country Special siblings in '68, Ford went all out to produce an eye-catching model with many non-stock features to reward two extremely successful sales districts.

The death of unique regional models lies more with the auto industry's systems of production than with any lack of interest on the part of dealer networks. The 1965 Mustang's list of optional powertrains, equipment and accessories, for instance, boggled the mind, and it was possible to build millions of cars without any identical twins. And that doesn't include all of the special order color combinations the factory would gladly create for a miniscule fee. The trend in Detroit since that heyday of personalization has been to eliminate options, to "package" related items as much as possible and to work as many features into the standard equipment list as possible. By 2001, Ford had reduced the entire Mustang line (not counting SVT's Cobra or Saleen's models) to approximately 50 possible order combinations based on engine choice (V-6 or V-8), transmission (five-speed manual or four-speed automatic), trim level (standard, deluxe or premium), and color (10 to choose from, no special orders accepted).

This effort to economize kept the Mustang's price tag at an acceptable level for buyers, but it ended any chance to own a modern factory-built custom, which led to an explosion of growth in the aftermarket industry.

Cars Not Found in this Chapter

Mustang legend tells of a 1968 **Sunshine Special** for the Florida Ford dealers, but historians have written it off as a no-show.

Nebraska allegedly received its own **Big Red Special** in 1970, but a single snapshot of a barn-bound red fastback is all that remains of this possible regional promotion.

High Country Specials

1966-68

Despite a strong national case of Mustang fever, sales slowdowns were starting to occur in certain parts of the country in early 1966. Whether the drop was due to market saturation or a weakening economy was not important to a group of Denver-area Ford dealers, who worked with Thurlo Newell in the district office to create one of the first—possibly *the* first—regional Mustang limited editions.

In July, 333 High Country Specials were built at the San Jose Ford plant and shipped to the 100 Denver dealers. The HCS was available with any '66 powertrain and body style, but in only one of three special colors: Aspen Gold, Columbine Blue, and Timberline Green. Dealer installed shield-shaped brass plaques (with sheetmetal screws!) that featured a horse galloping across high mountain tops were attached to the HCS front fenders. Because there were no exact specifications for placement of the badge, restorers have documented cars where the plaque sits above and ahead of the tri-bar running horse, and cars where the plaque rests above the "MUSTANG" lettering.

High Country Special plaques have held up well over the years because they are made of brass. *(Jerry Heasley)*

Placement of the HCS brass plaque differed from one dealership to the next. *(Jerry Heasley)*

The High Country Special in Denver was the first regional limited edition Mustang. *(Jerry Heasley)*

Denver area dealers made liberal use of newspaper advertisements to spread the word about High Country Specials. *(Don Hughmanick)*

Ads promoted the 1968's uniqueness, bragging "We lit it up, we scooped it and we added a spoiler." *(Don Hughmanick)*

Limited production of the HCS was again stressed in ads. *(Don Hughmanick)*

Ads stressed the High Country Special's unique colors. *(Don Hughmanick)*

This HCS is wearing the Columbine Blue paint scheme and optional wire wheel covers. *(Jerry Heasley)*

This newspaper report promoted the High Country Specials. *(Jerry Heasley)*

This '66 High Country Special was ordered with several interior upgrades. *(Jerry Heasley)*

32 • Mustang Special Editions

This HCS is decked out in Timberline Green and standard hubcaps. *(Jerry Heasley)*

This Aspen Gold coupe has several extra-cost features such as the luggage rack and styled-steel wheels. *(Jerry Heasley)*

Denver dealers must have benefited from the HCS editions because they raised the order for 1967 to 400 units. Again, the High Country Special could be ordered with any Mustang powertrain and body style. Aspen Gold, Columbine Blue, and Timberline Green were the only available colors, although records indicate the green was a slightly different mix from before.

In 1968 the Denver area received a uniquely styled High Country Special by way of its neighbors in California. Gone were the Colorado colors, and because the '68 HCS was based on the California Special, it could be had only as a coupe with a Shelby fiberglass decklid with integrated spoiler, fiberglass rear quarter extensions, sequential '65 Thunderbird taillights, a blacked-out grille (minus Mustang identification), a pop-off gas cap, fiberglass side scoops, Marchal or Lucas (depending on supply) foglamps, hood locks, and unique body striping.

Placing the HCS badge directly above the tri-bar was a popular choice at dealerships. *(Jerry Heasley)*

This '67 HCS has the Interior Decor group. *(Jerry Heasley)*

In its second year, the High Country Special was again offered in Columbine Blue, Timberline Green, or Aspen Gold (shown). *(Jerry Heasley)*

Foglamps adorned the front of each '68 HCS.
(Jerry Heasley)

Shelby-style tail lamps made the '68 HCS most distinctive visually.
(Jerry Heasley)

The 1968 High Country Special was a virtual clone of the California Special. *(Jerry Heasley)*

Twist locks were standard on the '68 High Country Special.
(Jerry Heasley)

This '68 HCS was heavily optioned, but customers could order them stripped, loaded, or anything in between.
(Jerry Heasley)

The '68 HCS had non-functional side scoops. *(Jerry Heasley)*

The '68 HCS and CS/GT wore thin-thick-thin stripes at the beltline. *(Jerry Heasley)*

Just like the GT/CS, the HCS could be ordered in any color and engine combination as other Mustangs. Wheel covers were the same ones used on 1968 GTs, but non-GTs had plain caps. Despite the eye-catching improvements—or perhaps because of them—HCS sales dropped in their final year to only 251 cars.

End-of-year figures showed that Mustang sales were beginning to cool off—if 607,568 cars in 1966 can be considered "slow." The decline would continue through 1967 (472,121) and 1968 (317,148).

THE FACTS

Model Year	1966-68
How Many Were Made?	333 (1966)
	400 (1967)
	251 (1968)
Engines	any Mustang engine
Reason for Limited Edition	to boost Mustang sales in Denver area
What Made It Special?	equipment level, Shelby look (1968)
Registries/Clubs	High Country Special Registry
	6874 Benton Court
	Arvada, CO 80003
	www.californiaspecial.com
Books	GT/California Special Recognition Guide & Owner's Manual (1988, Paul Newitt)

1967 Lone Star Limited

The economic boom that fueled Mustang sales in its first year was slowing by the time 1967 models debuted in late '66. Industry-wide auto sales would fall by one million units in '67, but the Mustang remained the top of its segment.

Mustang's standard equipment list was still respectable and enticing, featuring all Ford Motor Company safety equipment plus front bucket seats, full carpeting, floor-mounted shifter, vinyl interior trim, heater, wheel covers, and cigarette lighter.

To boost sales in the Dallas area, Ford dealers requested a special edition that in some way commemorated the state of Texas. What dealers received at the Dallas depot over a big barbecue dinner were 175 Lone Star Limited coupes painted Bluebonnet Blue (representing the state flower) with 200-cid six-cylinder or 289-cid V-8 engines. Each was equipped with that year's Sports Sprint package: wheel covers, chrome-plated air cleaner, rocker-panel molding, functional louvered hood, F70-14 Wide-Oval tires, and vinyl-covered shift lever (on automatics). The crowning touch, though, was a stylish Texas-shaped emblem with a running horse on each fender. After the party, the Bluebonnet Mustangs were driven or trucked back to their respective dealerships, where they sold quickly.

Based on the Sports Sprint package, the Lone Star Limited Mustang came only in Bluebonnet Blue. *(Jerry Heasley)*

History records that 173 of the Lone Star Limiteds were shipped with blue standard bucket seats, and 131 came with SelectAire air conditioning.

Restorers can verify the authenticity of a suspected Bluebonnet car by looking for the DSO numbers 61-5160 and a blank color code.

Total Mustang production for 1967 was 472,121 units. Ford managed to increase V-8 production by 20 percent for the year and, at the same time, special promotions boosted air conditioning installations to 16 percent, a 6.5 percent increase.

Lone Star Limited Mustangs received these special emblems. *(Jerry Heasley)*

This Lone Star Limited is one of the few survivors. Its owner has installed styled-steel wheels in place of the original stamped steel rims and full hubcaps. *(Jerry Heasley)*

Having an original dealer badge on a rare Mustang limited edition only adds to its nostalgic value. *(Jerry Heasley)*

Of the 175 Lone Star Limiteds built, 173 were shipped with this interior. *(Jerry Heasley)*

The Sports Sprint package came with the functional scooped hood and bright lower molding. *(Jerry Heasley)*

THE FACTS

Model Year	1967
How Many Were Made?	175
Engines	200-cid six-cylinder or 289-cid V-8
Reason for Limited Edition	to boost Mustang sales in Dallas region
What Made It Special?	specific color, special badge, equipment level
Registries/Clubs	www.limited600mustang.com
Books	*Mustang Production Guide, Vol. 2, 1967-73* (1994, Jim Smart and Jim Haskell)

1967 Ski Country Special

Denver was a beehive of Mustang activity in the late 1960s, as the mile-high Ford sales force never missed an opportunity to creatively market its cars.

In addition to its famous 1966-68 High Country Specials, the Greater Denver Ford Dealers assembled a colorful winter-theme package for its early 1967 Mustang, Fairlane, and Galaxie lines. Ski Country Specials were available in Aspen Red, Loveland Green, Vail Blue, Breckenridge Yellow, or Winter Park Turquoise—each representing a favorite Colorado ski destination and each originating from a variety of automakers!

Regardless of which Ford received it, the SCS option included a ski rack, limited-slip rear axle, two mounted snow tires, and the enigmatic "coffee bar" (most likely a console with built-in cupholders). An unpainted brass badge, shaped somewhat like the family crest that appeared on 1950s Fords, was attached to the SCS car's decklid (again with sheetmetal screws!).

Ads from the time suggest that the Ski Country Special package could not be ordered on the Mustang convertible.

Ads promoted Ski Country Special Galaxies as well as Mustangs. *(Don Hughmanick)*

This badge was affixed to the trunk lid of all Ski Country Specials. *(Don Hughmanick)*

THE FACTS

Model Year	1967
How Many Were Made?	n/a
Engines	all Mustang powerplants for 1967
Reason for Limited Edition	to associate Mustangs with local popular sport
What Made It Special?	badge, colors, unique accessories
Registries/Clubs	www.limited600mustang.com
Books	*Mustang Production Guide, Vol. 2, 1967-73* (1994, Jim Smart and Jim Haskell)

Indy Pacesetter 1967

Every Ford fan knows the 1964-1/2 Mustang led the field in that year's Indianapolis 500 race, and that the pony was tapped for those honors again in 1979 and 1994. So what is the deal with this Indy Pacesetter model that came out in 1967?

The distinction is that the 1964-1/2, '79, and '94 Mustangs (and their replicas) were considered "pace cars"; the 1967 model was simply a promotional special created by the Indianapolis area Ford dealer network. Pacesetters—robbing a revered name from defunct DeSoto—were regular coupes featuring a unique dual-band stripe that ran from the taillight almost all the way to the headlight at the level of the door handle. Reports indicate Pacesetter shift levers displayed a special badge or inscription, but little is known about these cars, otherwise.

Pacesetters were introduced in time to take advantage of the annual 500-mile Indy Memorial Day weekend event.

Little is known about the 1967 Pacesetter, and this Ford archive photo does not add to that knowledge. *(Don Hughmanick)*

THE FACTS

Model Year	1967
How Many Were Made?	n/a
Engines	n/a
Reason for Limited Edition	to promote sales in the Indianapolis area
What Made It Special?	unique stripe, coupe only
Registries/Clubs	www.limited600mustang.com
Books	*Mustang Production Guide, Vol. 2, 1967-73* (1994, Jim Smart and Jim Haskell)

1968 California Special

photo car owned by Joel Franckowiak

Working with its West Coast dealers, Ford produced 4,118 copies of its limited edition California Special—or GT/CS—from February through July. The coupe-only package was an attractive combination of Mustang GT and GT-350/500 parts based on Carroll Shelby's "Little Red" notchback prototype. In production form, the GT/CS wore a fiberglass decklid with a integrated spoiler (a Shelby piece), fiberglass rear quarter extensions, sequential '65 Thunderbird taillights (identical to the '68 Shelby units), a blacked-out grille (minus Mustang identification), a pop-off gas cap, fiberglass side scoops, Marchal or Lucas (depending on supply) foglamps, hood locks, unique body striping, and chrome "California Special" script on the rear quarters.

Any engine could be ordered with the California Special. *(Brad Bowling)*

The GT/CS borrowed its decklid, extensions, spoiler, taillights, and rear panel from Carroll Shelby's convertible GT-350/500. *(Brad Bowling)*

California got its very own Mustang in 1968—the GT/CS. *(Brad Bowling)*

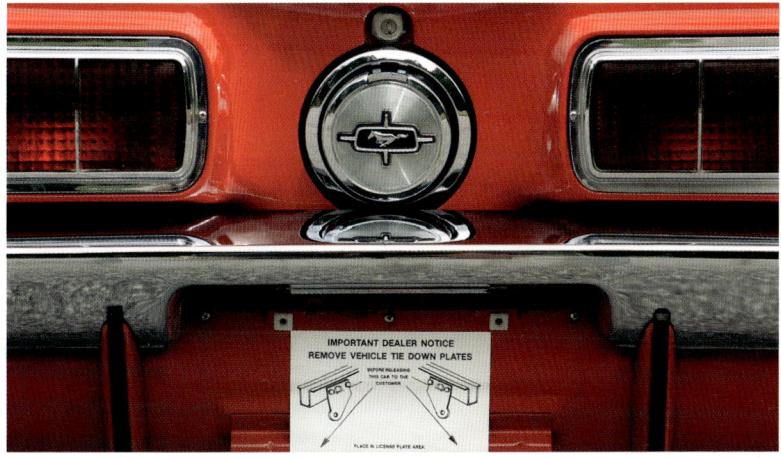
A pop-off gas cap was standard on the GT/CS. *(Brad Bowling)*

Chrome script was included in the GT/CS package. *(Brad Bowling)*

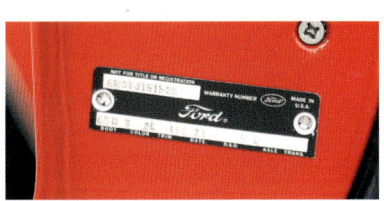
All California Special Mustangs were built in the San Jose plant. *(Brad Bowling)*

Side scoops were fitted with screen material to give the impression that they actually drew in air. *(Brad Bowling)*

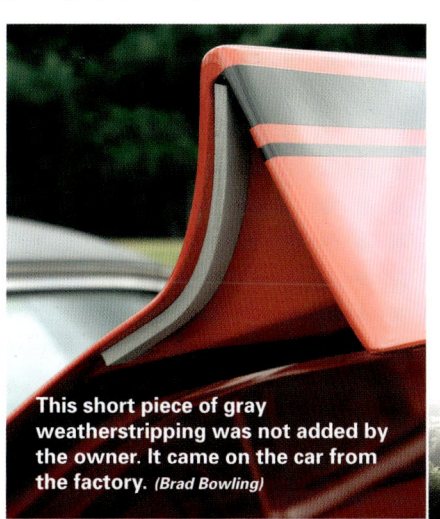
This short piece of gray weatherstripping was not added by the owner. It came on the car from the factory. *(Brad Bowling)*

Dual exhaust tips were not standard on California Specials. This one was ordered with the GT package. *(Brad Bowling)*

Louvered hoods were an extra-cost option for the California Special. *(Brad Bowling)*

The California Special was a sharp-looking coupe. *(Brad Bowling)*

California Specials could be ordered in any color and engine combination as other Mustangs. Wheelcovers were the same ones used on 1968 GTs. Sales fell short of the 5,500 Ford had estimated, but the faux Shelby styling made the GT/CS a popular collector car.

While the Mustang was still the best-selling pony car in America, it slipped from second place in domestic auto production in 1965 to seventh place in 1968. A 60-day strike against Ford from late September to late November of 1967 had a negative effect on Mustang sales and production.

Ford began installing latches on all its bucket seats in 1968 to prevent them from flopping forward under braking. *(Brad Bowling)*

THE FACTS

Model Year	1968
How Many Were Made?	4,118
Engines	any Mustang engine
Reason for Limited Edition	to boost Mustang sales in California
What Made It Special?	equipment level, Shelby look
Registries/Clubs	www.californiaspecial.com
Books	*GT/California Special Recognition Guide & Owner's Manual* (1988, Paul Newitt) *Mustang Production Guide, Vol. 2, 1967-73* (1994, Jim Smart and Jim Haskell)

Golden Nugget Special
1968

Were any of these Golden Nugget Specials ever built? *(Don Hughmanick)*

Ford dealers in Pacific Northwest states received a limited edition model in 1968 in the form of the Golden Nugget Mustang. Little has been documented about this rare pony, but an ad from the period declared that 525 Golden Nugget coupes would be shortly arriving at area dealerships with exclusive Sunlit Gold (color code Y) paint, black vinyl tops, black hood panels, black striping, whitewall tires, wheel covers, and a gold-colored plaque inscribed with the buyer's name.

Research has documented that all Golden Nugget Mustangs were built at the San Jose Ford factory (represented by an "R" in the VIN), then shipped to the Seattle district (74). Each GN Mustang will have the numbers "1111" following the Seattle DSO designation on the data plate.

It is not known if Ford built the advertised 525 GN Mustangs.

THE FACTS

Model Year	1968
How Many Were Made?	525 (advertised)
Engines	any Mustang engine
Reason for Limited Edition	to boost Mustang sales in Washington and Oregon
What Made It Special?	unique color, graphics
Registries/Clubs	www.1968mustang.org
Books	*Mustang Production Guide, Vol. 2, 1967-73* (1994, Jim Smart and Jim Haskell)

1968 Cardinal Edition

Neighboring states Virginia and North Carolina shared a one-year appearance package in 1968 known as the Cardinal Edition. Named for the two states' official bird (they also share the dogwood as a state flower), the Cardinal Edition was advertised as a Candyapple Red (T code) coupe with 200-cid six-cylinder power (T), black interior, flip-open gas cap, GT stripe, chrome wheel lip molding, wheel covers, and a diamond-shaped emblem sporting the head of a Cardinal on the sail pillar.

Of course, dealers promoted the long list of Mustang options that could be applied to the CE, so it appears that anything short of a body style change was possible. More than one CE has been uncovered with V-8 power. It is not known how long the CE campaign lasted, but advertising appears to have started around the end of March.

Because Candyapple Red was a regular color option in 1968, there is no easy way to determine the authenticity of a suspected CE other than through original documentation. All Cardinal Edition coupes will show a DSO of 25 (Richmond) on their data plates.

The Cardinal Edition Mustang was a one-year-only special. *(Don Hughmanick)*

THE FACTS

Model Year	1968
How Many Were Made?	n/a
Engines	any Mustang engine
Reason for Limited Edition	to boost Mustang sales in Virginia and North Carolina
What Made It Special?	unique color, graphics
Registries/Clubs	www.1968mustang.org
Books	*Mustang Production Guide, Vol. 2, 1967-73* (1994, Jim Smart and Jim Haskell)

Limited Edition 600

photo car owned by Don Hughmanick

Proliferation was Ford's plan for 1969, a year in which the company offered an array of engines and speed packages the likes of which Detroit will never see again.

Mustangs were available with two six-cylinders (a 200-cid T-code version and a 250-cid L-code) or one of eight V-8s: an "economy" 302-cid unit (F), the awesome 302-cid Boss motor (G), a 351-cid Windsor (H), a 351-cid four-barrel (M), a final-year 390-cid (S), a 428-cid Cobra Jet (Q), a 428-cid Super Cobra Jet (R), and the ground-pounding 429-cid Boss plant (Z). Ford's stable during this period included the Mach 1, GT, Boss 302, Boss 429, Shelby GT-350, and Shelby GT-500—all high-performance models built from the same basic platform.

The new-for-1969 Mustang grew substantially to accommodate the larger powerplants. Wheelbase remained unchanged at 108 inches, but overall length grew by 3.8 inches. The windshield was raked more steeply than the 1968 model, making the Mustang's profile sleeker than ever. Four round headlamps sat at the front of the car for the first, and only, time—the outer lenses deeply recessed in the front fender openings and the inboard units set into the grille ends.

For 1969 designers eliminated the indented cove that had visually pinched the Mustang's waist since the 1965 model, but they replaced it with a feature line that ran from the tip of the front fender to just behind the rear door seam. Non-functional air vents sat just in front of the rear wheel opening on coupes and convertibles, and fastbacks featured a backwards C-shaped scoop. The "SportsRoof" top was 0.9 inches lower than it had been on previous fastbacks, and

All 600s came with the base hubcaps unless otherwise upgraded. *(Brad Bowling)*

Records suggest that four out of five Limited Edition 600s were painted Flower Power Red. *(Brad Bowling)*

Unlike some special editions, the 600 could be ordered in a variety of ways. *(Brad Bowling)*

a small rear window abutted the glass door and provided some coupe-like visibility to the rear passengers.

The coupe received its own dress-up package in 1969 known as the Grandé, which included a vinyl roof, plush interior, deluxe two-spoke steering wheel, color-keyed racing mirrors, full wheelcovers, electric clock, bright exterior body moldings, dual outside paint stripes, and luxury foam bucket seats—all for only $231 above the normal hardtop with comparable equipment.

The once-popular GT Equipment Group, which would be eliminated at the end of 1969, was available on any body style for an extra $147. The base GT engine was a 351-cid Windsor V-8 with 250 horsepower, and the package included special handling equipment, lower body racing stripes, dual exhausts, pin-type hood lock latches, simulated hood scoop with integral turn signal indicators (shaker scoop with the 428CJ Ram Air V-8), three-speed manual transmission, four-wheel drum brakes, glass-belted white sidewall tires, and styled steel wheels with Argent Silver trim and GT hubcaps. The GT Equipment Group was not available on Grandé coupes, six-cylinder engines or the base 302.

The most popular Mustang upgrade package in history, the SportsRoof-based Mach 1, debuted in 1969. It came standard with a matte black hood, simulated hood scoop and exposed NASCAR-style hood lock pins, which could be deleted. A spoiler, available after the Boss 302 introduction in January, cost extra. A reflective side stripe and rear stripes carried the model designation just behind the front wheel arches, and above the chrome pop-up gas cap. Chrome styled steel wheels and chrome exhausts tips (when optional four-barrel carburetors were ordered) were other bright touches. Also featured were dual color-keyed racing mirrors, and a handling suspension. Mach 1s also had the fanciest interior appointments, with high-back bucket seats; black carpets; a Rim-Blow steering wheel; center console; clock; sound-deadening insulation; and

The 600 fender decal was the most obvious piece of limited edition identification. *(Don Hughmanick)*

teakwood-grained trim on the doors, dash and console. Base engine was a 351-cid two-barrel Windsor V-8. This was essentially a stroked 302-cid Ford V-8 with raised deck height, which created a great street performance engine. Options included the 351-cid 290-hp four-barrel V-8 and a 390-cid 320-hp V-8.

The awesome Cobra Jet 428-cid V-8 engine introduced midway through the '68 season once again made an appearance on the Mustang option list. It was available with either the GT or Mach 1 package in Cobra Jet (CJ-428) or Super Cobra Jet (SCJ-428) form. The base Cobra Jet generated 335 hp at 5200 rpm and 440 lbs.-ft. of torque at 3400 rpm, while the SCJ was the same engine with Ram Air induction, a hardened steel cast crankshaft, special "LeMans" connecting rods and improved balancing for drag racing. It had the same advertised horsepower but was, in reality, more powerful.

According to Don Hughmanick and his well-presented Web site, www.limited600mustang.com, Philadelphia-area Ford dealers took the company's national "Mustang Stampede" promotion in May of 1969 one step further and created their own Limited Edition 600. Named for the number of units they hoped to move of the highly advertised special model, all 600s were ordered with a

The 600 package included the non-functional hood scoop, but the hood pins on this photo car were added by an owner.
(Brad Bowling)

The rope around the 600 decal suggests a tie-in with Ford's national "Mustang Stampede" promotion. *(Brad Bowling)*

Sports Appearance Group that included a non-functional hood scoop (with integral turn signals), full wheel covers, E78x14 whitewall tires, chrome remote driver's-side mirror, AM radio, special "Limited Edition 600" fender decals, and multi-colored tape pinstripes that ran from the headlight bucket to the side scoop.

Advertising boasted, "You can be only one of 600 people to own one of these specially equipped Mustangs in the country." As with many of the spring promotions from Ford, the point was to create excitement and to increase foot traffic down at the local dealer during what is traditionally a slow sales time.

Only coupes and fastbacks could be ordered as 600s. Some coupes were shipped with vinyl tops, some went bare, and one Mach 1 crept into the mix. Flower Power Red (special order code WT5185) and Groovy Green (MX8241928) were the only two colors available for the 600 model—the former was a match for 1965 Poppy Red and '70 Calypso Coral, and the latter would be seen again as '72 Bright Lime. Pinstripes for the red car were white-gold-white, while the green cars wore black-red-black lines along their flanks. Hughmanick's research suggests all 600s received base black interiors, but records do not verify this educated guess.

Most 600s were built with six-cylinder engines, but some 302s and a single two-barrel 351 were shipped as well. The entire 600 run was produced between April 21 and 29 at the Metuchen, New Jersey, Ford plant. Falling a bit short of their goal, the Philadelphia sales group only ordered 503 of its Limited Edition 600s, most of which are believed to be Flower Power Red. Mustang 600 buyers could outfit their cars with any regular options, but it is believed most dealers ordered them with an eye toward keeping the sticker low.

Like many regional Mustang promotions in the 1960s, the 600 was introduced with a big invitation-only party

All 600s were built in the Metuchen Ford plant. (Brad Bowling)

(Brad Bowling)

and drive-away for participating dealers. Philadelphia District Manager Jack Mandell arrived by helicopter at the Flying W, a local dude ranch, where he mounted a horse, charged across the airport grounds and greeted partygoers while decked out in western kit to kick off his district's contribution to the "Mustang Stampede."

For a 1969 Mustang to be one of the rare Limited Edition 600s, it must have a DSO of 16 (Philadelphia district), followed immediately by the numbers 2783, 2784, 2785, 2786, 2787, or 2788. The color code on the data plate will be blank, but the buck tag near the passenger-side hood hinge will indicate special paint and list WT5185 (Flower Power Red) or MX8241928 (Groovy Green).

Of the 299,824 Mustangs produced in 1969, 81.5 percent were ordered with V-8 engines, and automatic transmissions accounted for 71 percent of the herd.

THE FACTS

Model Year	1969
How Many Were Made?	503
Engines	both six-cylinders, both 302 V-8s and two-barrel 351-cid V-8
Reason for Limited Edition	to boost spring sales with national "Mustang Stampede"
What Made It Special?	unique colors, badge
Registries/Clubs	www.limited600mustang.com

1970 ARI/Twister Specials

photo car owned by Gary Pietraniec (green ARI pace car)
photo car owned by Walt Wise (Twister Special)

Ford rested on its automotive laurels in 1970, having delivered to Mustang fans a dizzying array of performance and cosmetic packages the year before. The '70 model received only minor changes—mostly cosmetic—such as the new single headlamps located inside a wider grille flanked by simulated air intakes and a restyled tail lamp panel.

The 1970 Mustang lost the side-mounted fake air intakes at the rear of each door that had been so prominent on the '69, and the front fender-mounted reflector grew larger and was oriented vertically above the bumper line.

Black honeycomb trim dressed up the rear of the Mach 1, and ribbed aluminum rocker panel moldings (with Mach 1 call-outs) visually lowered the middle of the fastback-only package. A fake scoop became standard equipment on the Mach 1 hood (although a true shaker was available with the 351-cid V-8), as did a black stripe and twist-in pins.

The GT Equipment option was gone in 1970, but the stylish, coupe-only Grandé package returned for a second year. The Boss twins once again set the standard for high-performance Mustangs, though for their final year of production.

Unfortunately for Ford, there was a plethora of new competition for the Mustang in 1970—the redesigned Plymouth Barracuda, Chevrolet Camaro, Pontiac Firebird,

The ARI convertibles received VIP-friendly options such as air conditioning and deluxe interiors. *(Jerry Heasley)*

All ARI convertibles had 428CJ engines upgraded for greater performance and durability. *(Jerry Heasley)*

Even nearsighted fans could tell what engine powered the ARI pace cars. *(Jerry Heasley)*

This green 1970 Mustang convertible was built to be the official pace car of Michigan International Speedway. *(Jerry Heasley)*

and Dodge's appropriately named Challenger, to name a few—so the company was very much open to promotion ideas from the field. This receptiveness and a canceled promotional opportunity led to the creation of that year's most colorful fleet of limited edition Mustangs.

Late in 1969 Ford had contracted to build some promotional Mustangs (five convertibles, and perhaps as many as five Mach 1s) for American Raceways Inc. (ARI), a five-track network comprised of Atlanta International Raceway, Eastern International Speedway (under construction), Texas International Speedway, Riverside International Raceway, and Michigan International Speedway. With a graphics package designed by Boss 302 stylist Larry Shinoda, production of the heavily optioned convertibles began on October 17. Each car was identically equipped with a R-code 428 Cobra Jet engine, air conditioning, and other VIP-friendly accessories—the only exception being a fuel evaporative system for the Texas-bound pace car.

After rolling off the Dearborn assembly line they were shipped to Ford's "IR Building Garage," then on to an outside shop where modifications were made in the interest of durability and improved performance. The 428CJ powerplants were balanced and blueprinted at Ford Engineering, which was also responsible for giving the heads a three-angle valve job and shot-peening the stock rods, among other mods. Engine oil coolers (standard on the Super Cobra Jet Drag Pack) were installed for greater resistance to race-duty heat. The stock CJ oil pan was modified to hold eight quarts with baffles to prevent starvation on the banked ovals.

Rollbars made from padded 1.5-inch tubing and a 150-psi Stewart-Warner oil pressure gauge were added to the interiors. For more stability at pace speeds, each convertible was lowered by torching one wind of coil from each of the front springs.

Ford was proud of its ARI pace cars, going so far as to brag about them in magazine ads with taglines such as: "Get the Mustang Pace Car specials...hot off the track!". Unfortunately for its investment, ARI declared bankruptcy just after the convertibles and Mach 1s were delivered. During this same period, by sheer coincidence, representatives of the Kansas City District Sales Office requested a special batch of 100 1970 Mustang Mach 1s and the same number of Torinos to display when Ford's Total Performance Day traveling exhibit visited the area on November 7, 1969. Their timing brought about the now-famous Twister Special promotion, the idea being that each Mustang would sport a Super Cobra Jet 428-cid V-8 and every Torino would be fitted with the SCJ version of Ford's 429-cid V-8.

Ford was able to recycle the ARI graphics package, but inserted a funnel cloud image in place of the original racetrack logo. Twister Special Mustangs were painted Grabber Orange (U code) with black decals; Torinos were Vermillion and had similar graphics. A shortage of 428-cid engines at the Dearborn plant meant a last-minute switch, and half of the Mustangs were delivered with 351-cid four-barrel (M) powerplants (but with the big-block's reinforced shock towers).

Unlike other regional special edition Mustangs, the Twisters were produced with a set list of features, the only deviations being for transmission choice. The original KC request was to split the automatic/manual transmission ratio exactly in half, but the final product ran heavier on C-6 Cruise-O-Matics than four-speeds. There were 24 automatics in the 428 cars, 39 in the 351 Mustangs, 24 four-speeds installed in 428 cars, and only nine four-speeds hooked up to the 351 Mach 1s.

The Kansas City version of Total Performance Day in 1970 sounds like an automotive Woodstock, with speed guru Bob Tasca giving a seminar on musclecars, the three top racing mechanics in the country showing how to convert a production car to a race car, a slalom contest, and a drag racing exhibition by Hubert Platt. Trophies were awarded to the day's competitors by Miss Cobra and Miss Mach 1.

In the midst of all the action was a static display of 96 Twister Special Mustangs and 90 Twister Special Torinos (a KC contractor had applied the unique decals), all of which were driven to their receiving dealerships and sold to the public.

All Twister Specials were painted Grabber Orange. *(Jerry Heasley)*

Enthusiasts today seem to know more about the Twisters than other regional limited edition Mustangs, and apparently they have preserved them in high numbers, although there were relatively few of them built. According to Jim Smart and Jim Haskell's *Mustang Production Guide, Volume 2*, the Twister Special Registry has located 48 of the original cars—that's half the production run!

The graphics package is the only unique component of the Twister Special Mustang, and those decals are available today in reproduction form through the aftermarket. It is not a genuine Twister if it is not a Mach 1 (body code 63C) in Grabber Orange from the Dearborn plant (F code) with the 428 or 351 engines, all of which can be determined by examining the car's original certification label on the driver's door jamb. The 96 Twisters were built in a batch, which means they were assigned consecutive six-digit serial numbers—in this case beginning with "118."

Despite the successful KC promotion the slow Mustang sales decline continued. A total of 190,727 1970 Mustangs were built—a drop of 100,000 from 1969. 1970 marked the final year of production for the awesome 428

Half of the Twister Special Mustangs were equipped with stock 428-cid Super Cobra Jet engines (shown).
(Jerry Heasley)

Twister Special buyers only had two choices to make: engine (351 or 428) and transmission (manual or automatic).
(Jerry Heasley)

Cobra Jet and Super Cobra Jet engines, with 2,817 (in 1968), 13,193 (1969), and 2,671 (1970) of the big-blocks being fitted into all body styles of Mustang, according to the 428 Cobra Jet Registry.

THE FACTS

ARI Pace Cars
Model Year	1970
How Many Were Made?	(convertibles) 5, (Mach 1s, est.) 5
Engine	428-cid SCJ V-8
Reason for Limited Edition	to have high-profile pace cars at NASCAR race tracks
What Made It Special?	engine mods, decals
Registries/Clubs	428 Cobra Jet Registry
	Gary B. Pietraniec
	6890 Plainfield
	Dearborn, MI 48217

Twister Specials
Model Year	1970
How Many Were Made?	96
Engines	351-cid/4V V-8 and 428-cid SCJ V-8
Reason for Limited Edition	to give Kansas City its own performance model
What Made It Special?	Mach 1 equipment, decals
Registries/Clubs	Twister Special Registry
	7520 NW Rochester
	Topeka, KS 66617
	www.mustanggt.org
Books	*Mustang Production Guide, Vol. 2, 1967-73* (1994, Jim Smart and Jim Haskell)

Sidewinder Special 1970

It might seem strange to name the 1970 Sidewinder Special Mustang after a poisonous snake found nowhere near the Iowa and Nebraska dealerships that distributed it. The other odd thing about the Sidewinder is how little information can be found about the estimated 40 cars sold, even though several are still in existence.

David Charlier's online registry, which has made a valiant attempt to track the elusive serpent, reports that all cars in its files are Dearborn-built fastbacks with 351-cid V-8 four-barrel (M code) engines available in a variety of stock Mustang colors originally shipped to the Omaha (54) district sales office.

The only unique characteristic of this Midwestern model is a large Twister-style logo on the rear quarter panel of a stylized snake with dragster-like wheels and the word "Sidewinder" (quote marks included) next to it. It appears the ARI/Twister side stripe was used, as well.

The logo is amateurishly rendered, leading some to speculate that the Sidewinder may have been a decal kit sold to Iowa and Nebraska dealers, and not part of a regional promotion.

Not much is known about the 1970 Sidewinder Special.
(David Charlier)

The ARI/Twister stripes are clearly visible in this photo.
(Don Hughmanick)

THE FACTS

Model Year	1970
How Many Were Made?	40 (est.)
Engine	351-cid/4V V-8
Reason for Limited Edition	unknown
What Made It Special?	decals
Registries/Clubs	http://people.freenet.de/pony/sidewinder.htm
Books	*Mustang Production Guide, Vol. 2, 1967-73* (1994, Jim Smart and Jim Haskell)

1985 Twister II

photo car owned by Monty Seawright

The Mustang's performance image received a boost in 1985 when an available engine broke the 200-horsepower barrier for the first time in 12 years. Getting an advertised 210 horses out of the GT's 5.0-liter V-8 was the result of old-fashioned hot rod tricks and new technology—low-friction roller tappets, a high-performance camshaft, stainless steel headers that replaced "high-flow" cast-iron manifolds and twin exhaust pipes purging the hot exhaust gases through individual catalytic converters. Lost horsepower was reclaimed through a new accessory drive system that reduced to half speed the air conditioner compressor, power steering pump, and alternator.

When mated to the four-speed automatic overdrive transmission, the 5.0-liter lost its carburetor—along with 45 horsepower—and claimed an output of 165 horses. GT improvements included a T-5 transmission with shorter gear throws, a quad-shock system in the rear, a larger rear stabilizer bar, and Goodyear Eagle P225/60VR-15 "Gatorback" unidirectional tires mounted on new alloy wheels.

The 3.8-liter V-6 with electronic fuel injection soldiered on with 120 horsepower in 1985; the 2.3-liter four-cylinder with single-barrel carburetor was rated at 88.

Ford dropped the base L series, creating an entry-level package out of the LX with standard power brakes and steering; remote-control right-side mirror; dual-note horn; interval windshield wipers; and an AM/FM stereo radio. As before, both notchback and hatchback bodies were offered. New standard interior features included a console; low-back bucket seats (on LX); articulated sport seats (on GT); luxury door trim panels; and covered visor mirrors. The convertible's quarter trim panels were revised to accommodate a refined seatbelt system. Mechanical radio faces switched to a contemporary flat design. All Mustangs had larger tires this year, with added urethane lower body side protection. A new electronic AM/FM stereo radio with cassette player was added to the options list. Both the 3.8-liter V-6 and 5.0-liter V-8 had a new oil warning light.

The Mustang received a new front cap design with an airdam below the bumper. The grille was similar to what the SVO wore—one wide slot with angled sides in a sloping front panel with a Ford oval emblem affixed just below the hood line. On GTs the airdam held integral foglamps. Full-width tail lamps broke only for the license plate opening, with backup lenses sitting high in each inner section and a Ford oval posted on the right side of the trunk lid. Exterior trim and accents changed from earlier models' charcoal to black, except for the horizontal rub strip. The GT received a unique tape treatment on the hood.

These 10-spoke wheels were new for 1985, and were available only on the Mustangs with V-8 power. *(Brad Bowling)*

This image is known as the "tornado with eyes." *(Brad Bowling)*

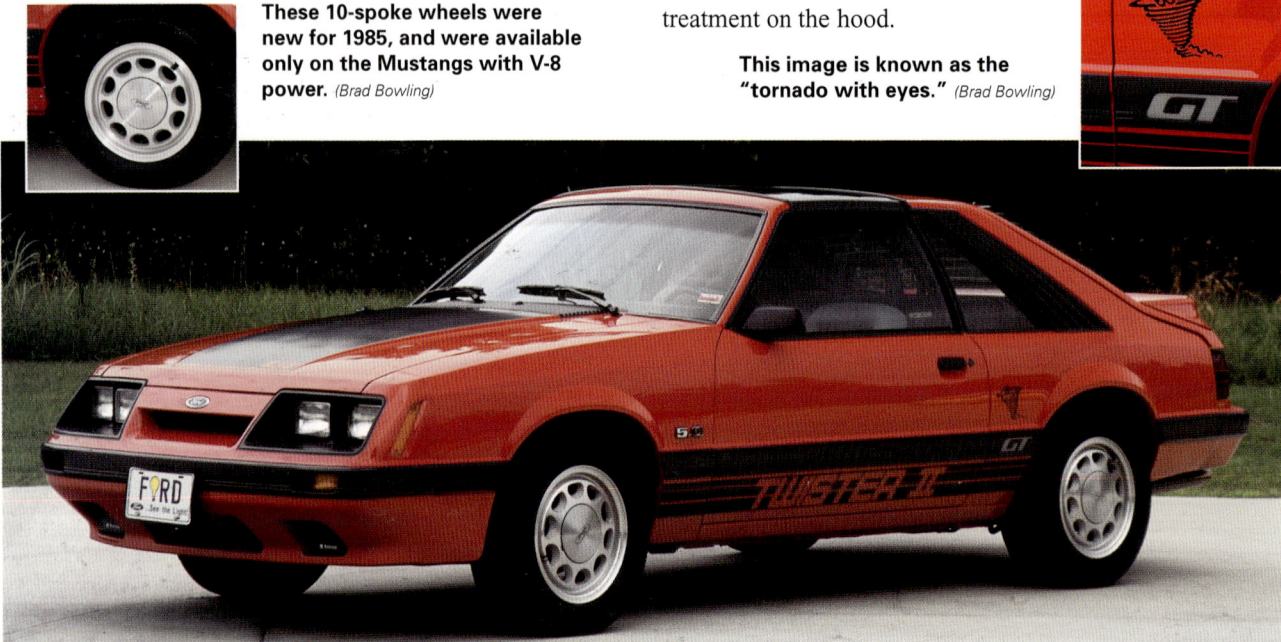

In 1985 Ford worked with the Kansas City sales district to produce 90 Twister II Mustangs. *(Brad Bowling)*

Package-specific decals separate the Twister II from regular GTs. *(Brad Bowling)*

Other than decals and a DSO, the Twister II is like any other 1985 GT. *(Brad Bowling)*

In Ford's Kansas City sales district, someone noticed that 1985 marked the 15th anniversary of the fondly remembered 1970 Twister Special—that Mach 1-based limited edition whose clever name referred to the area's propensity for deadly tornadoes (see the earlier entry in this book for more information). Collaborating with Ford Motor Company again, Kansas City dealers arranged to purchase 90 GTs in hatchback and convertible form and apply certain commemorative decals as part of a "Twister II" promotion.

Being a cosmetic package, dealers were free to order the cars with any combination of colors, powerplants, and options that would normally be available on the GT. According to research undertaken by David and Kathy Bowers at www.mustanggt.org, Twister II GTs were assembled during October of 1984 with vehicle identification numbers falling somewhere between 109800-109899, 110300-110399, and 112200-112299. The majority were painted Jalapena Red (code 2R), but Oxford White (9L), Medium Canyon Red Metallic (2A), and possibly Silver Metallic (1E) were also offered.

Along with the rocker panel "TWISTER II" striping and "tornado with eyes" funnel cloud insignia, the package included a bronze dash plate (not all Twister IIs received the plaques due to sales staff members with sticky fingers); an alabaster coaster with a running horse logo and "1985 Limited Edition TWISTER II, Kansas City District, October 1984" lettering (many of these coasters also went missing); and a press kit from Ford discussing the promotion (quite a few of these never reached...well, you know the rest).

All Twister IIs have a DSO number of 53 (indicating Kansas City) on their certification label and build sheet, but the Ford window sticker does not mention anything about the package.

According to the Bowerses, 74 Twister IIs were five-speed hatchbacks, two were automatic-equipped hatchbacks, nine were five-speed convertibles, and five were automatic convertibles. A dozen or so Twister IIs were ordered with the optional 3.08:1 rear axle gears, but no convertibles were so equipped.

The Twister II made its debut alongside several 1970 models during a luncheon at the Marriott Hotel in Overland Park, Kansas, in November of 1984.

As Ford hoped, the excitement generated by all of Ford's performance models had a positive effect on sales. The public eagerly bought 156,514 Mustangs in 1985 (Ford had forecast sales in the 128,000 range), 31.7 percent of which were equipped with 5.0-liter V-8 engines.

THE FACTS

Model Year	1985
How Many Were Made?	90
Engine	5.0-liter V-8
Reason for Limited Edition	commemorate 15th anniversary of Twister Special
What Made It Special?	graphics
Registries/Clubs	www.mustanggt.org www.themustangsource.com

1987 Ford Motorsport Nationals Special Edition

When the Mustang received its first significant restyling since 1979, no one outside of Ford could have predicted the new look would run with very little change for the next seven years! This unprecedented longevity would not have been necessary, but Ford had plans to replace the Mustang's traditional rear-drive with a Mazda-designed front-driver. A revolt among its planners and the general public halted that scheme.

The 1987 revamp included new front and rear body fascias, aero headlamps, and a prominent lower feature line accented with heavy moldings. Wind tunnel work had sculpted the Mustang into a smooth brick, with the base hatchback registering a 0.36 drag coefficient (compared to the '79's 0.44) and the bulky GT three-door turning out a 0.38. Changes to the Mustang interior included a redesigned instrument panel that created a roomier passenger compartment, pod-mounted headlamp switches, and a center console.

The new Mustang retained a 100.5-inch wheelbase and 179-inch overall length. It was 68.3 inches wide and about 52 inches high (depending on body style) with a track of 56.6 inches in the front and 57 inches in the rear. Weights for various models ranged from 2,724 pounds (base coupe) to 3,214 pounds (GT convertible), roughly a 100-pound increase model-to-model over 1986 specs.

The standard engine in the base LX model notchbacks, hatchbacks, and convertibles was the ubiquitous 2.3-liter four, improved for 1987 with a new multi-port fuel-injection system. Its output was up slightly to 90 hp and 130 lbs.-ft. of torque. Optional in LX models and standard in GTs was a 225-hp 5.0-liter V-8. Its 25-hp gain was the result of a return to a pre-1986 cylinder head design. The V-6 and turbocharged four from 1986 were no longer offered. The SVO was gone, but the LX coupe with the 5.0-liter H.O. V-8 seemed nearly as exciting to speed freaks on a budget.

Red, white and blue '87 GT hatchbacks made a patriotic display at the Ford Motorsport Nationals near Reading, Pa. *(Don Hughmanick)*

Also gone were the myriad choices of powerplant and model combinations. Both 1987 Mustang engines came with either a five-speed manual transmission or an optional automatic overdrive transmission. Other technical features included vented disc brakes in front, rear drum brakes, and a modified MacPherson strut front suspension with coil springs. The rear suspension featured a live axle with links and coil springs.

The convertible, priced at under $13,000 in LX form (or less than $16,000 as a GT), received a lot of attention—about one out of every eight '87 Mustangs were ragtops. Total model year production was 159,145 units for 1987, noticeably down from 1986, and industry analysts were ready to write off the Mustang as an "old" rear-drive car that had had its day. Mustang sales were only beginning to take off again, which would disprove the predictions of an early demise. Since the Mustang's major development and tooling costs had already been absorbed, it wound up generating extremely good profits. Ford would maintain it, without any major alterations, all the way through the end of model year 1993.

One of many events to promote the '87 models took place at the Maple Grove Raceway in Reading, Pa., during Ford's third annual Motorsport Nationals on June 6 and 7. Sponsored by the Quality Plus Ford Dealers of the Philadelphia District, the Nationals included drag racing, a car show, swap meet, Bigfoot monster truck demonstration, and a new car show.

To create its own patriotic display, the dealers put in a combined order for red, white, and blue Mustang GT hatchbacks. Don Hughmanick, who has researched the event for his Web site, reports there were approximately 30 to 40 of each color, and that cars were equipped with various preferred equipment packages based on the ordering dealer's choosing. The only distinguishing feature

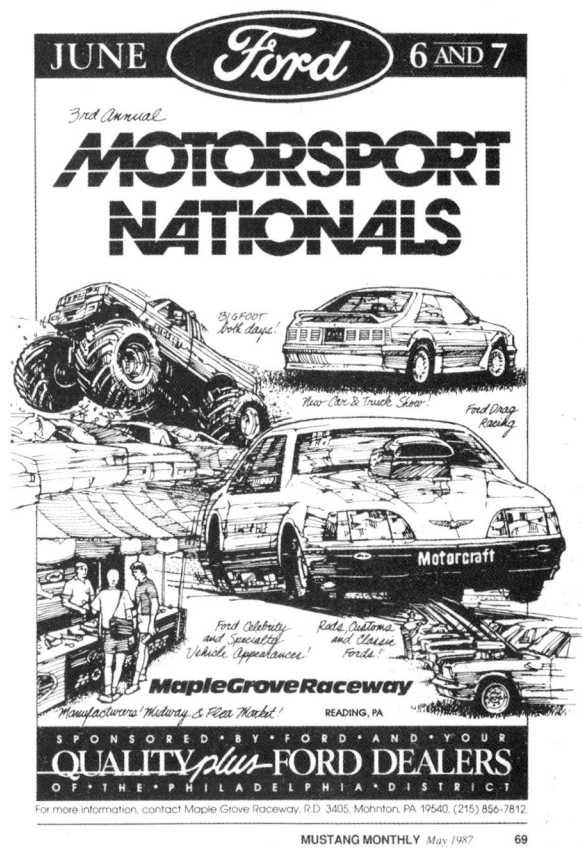

Philadelphia-area Ford dealers put on quite a show for their potential customers. *(Don Hughmanick)*

was a square decal on the front of each fender reading "Ford Motorsport Nationals Special Edition." At the end of the all-Ford weekend, dealers drove the GTs back to their showrooms and touted their special status to potential customers.

Hughmanick reports a similar promotional event in the Philadelphia area in 1993 using a number of white Limited Edition convertibles.

THE FACTS

Model Year	1987
How Many Were Made?	n/a
Engine	5.0-liter V-8
Reason for Limited Edition	promote Ford Motorsport Nationals at Maple Grove Raceway
What Made It Special?	fender decal
Registries/Clubs	www.limited600mustang.com

1989
25th Anniversary Carolina Ford Dealers

photo car owned by Monty Seawright

In a fit of profound negligence, Ford Motor Company did not produce a special edition to commemorate the silver anniversary of its world-famous Mustang.

Going into 1989, fans watched with bated breath as two revered Mustang powerhouses—Jack Roush and Steve Saleen—developed prototypes that promised to get the official nod from Ford. Roush' concept was an awesome limited-production hatchback whose 351-cid V-8 and twin turbochargers cranked out 400 horsepower. Saleen's contender, though never advertised as an anniversary special, became the 300-horsepower all-white hatchback—161 of which were built and sold.

There are many theories to explain this appalling oversight. When asked why it had pie on its corporate face, Ford's public relations people suggested the 25th anniversary would *not* take place on April 17, 1989 (25 years to the day since the Mustang's introduction), but at the start of the 1990 model year. Since Ford released its 20th anniversary car in April of '84, this was a difficult argument to make. Another, more plausible, explanation lies in the fact that Ford had intended to kill the traditional

All Carolina Ford Dealers 25th Anniversary Mustangs were equipped with the popular 5.0-liter V-8. *(Brad Bowling)*

Ford began installing its mass airflow sensor system on all V-8 Mustangs starting in 1989. The device had debuted in '88 on cars bound for the California market. *(Brad Bowling)*

CFD anniversary cars were simple and clean. *(Brad Bowling)*

56 • Mustang Special Editions

Custom floormats were part of the CFD anniversary package. They were installed at the dealerships. *(Brad Bowling)*

This window sticker was added at the dealerships. *(Brad Bowling)*

CFD anniversary cars were ordered with Scarlet Red cloth interiors *(above)*. *(Brad Bowling)*

Anniversary cars received the standard 5.0-liter LX wheels and tires. *(Brad Bowling)*

rear-drive Mustang platform shortly after the '89 model year and was not devoting funds to a model scheduled for extinction.

Despite the ignored birthday, Mustang enthusiasts had plenty to be happy about. Base Mustang LXs still came with the 2.3-liter four-cylinder engine, a five-speed manual transmission, power front disc brakes, modified MacPherson strut suspension, 20.0:1-ratio rack-and-pinion power steering, styled road wheels, and P195/75R-14 black sidewall steel-belted radial tires. Comfortable interiors with cloth reclining seats were standard. The three-model line had list prices from $9,050 to $17,512, and with the optional Special Value Group buyers got power locks, dual electric mirrors, an electronic AM/FM stereo with a cassette tape player, and more.

The top-of-the-line GT hatchback ($13,272) and convertible ($17,512) added such treats as aero body upgrades, the 225-hp 5.0-liter H.O. V-8, a five-speed manual transmission with overdrive fifth gear, 14.7:1 ratio power rack-and-pinion steering, a taut handling suspension system, and P225/60VR-15 unidirectional Goodyear Eagle

These red decals were the most obvious indicator of anniversary status. *(Brad Bowling)*

The convertible top has never been lowered on this pampered CFD anniversary car. *(Brad Bowling)*

The red tape applied to the body molding was a standard LX feature. *(Brad Bowling)*

All CFD convertibles were ordered with white tops. *(Brad Bowling)*

tires on 15-inch diameter 16-spoke cast aluminum wheels. Starting in 1989, all V-8 Mustangs sold in the United States were equipped with mass airflow sensors introduced the previous year on California-bound cars.

The GT suspension was really a piece of high-tech work, with gas-pressurized hydraulic struts, variable-rate coil springs, and a stabilizer bar up front. The rear also featured variable-rate coils plus a Quadra-shock setup with vertically-mounted gas-pressurized shock absorbers, horizontally-mounted, freon-filled axle dampers, and a fat stabilizer bar. A new LX 5.0-L Sport series combined the entry-level model, 5.0-liter V-8 and the GT's multi-adjustable seats. Prices started at $11,410 for the coupe and reached $17,001 for the convertible.

With the news that no anniversary model was coming, several Ford dealer networks around the country created special editions from existing stock with specific colors and some tape stripes. One of the more tasteful packages, known simply as the 25th Anniversary Mustang, was developed by the Carolina Ford Dealers.

All CFD anniversary cars were painted Oxford White (code 9L) with Scarlet Red (D) cloth interiors. They were equipped with 5.0-liter V-8 engines, but buyers could choose between the five-speed manual and automatic overdrive four-speed transmissions. Body styles were limited to the convertible and hatchback LX models, but any LX option could be applied to the limited edition.

Each CFD car received unique "25th Anniversary Edition" red graphics on the lower part of the door, custom red floormats, and a special commemorative keychain—all of which were added at the dealerships.

According to existing records, the Carolina Ford Dealers ordered 500 white Mustangs to sell as limited editions, but there is currently no breakout as to body styles and transmissions. All CFD 25th Anniversary Editions will have a DSO of 22 (Charlotte).

THE FACTS

Model Year	1989
How Many Were Made?	(advertised) 500
Engine	5.0-liter V-8
Reason for Limited Edition	to commemorate Mustang anniversary in Carolinas
What Made It Special?	equipment level, decals, color

SECTION 4:

Dealership Promotions

Motivated dealerships have always been a good source of special edition cars, although the numbers tend to be quite low (often in the single digits) and documentation often disappears after a few years.

Creating a batch of XYZ Special Edition Mustangs for the ABC Ford dealer in the 1960s was a simple matter of turning in the same completed options list several times, getting a plug in the local newspaper, and changing some text in the weekly advertising campaign. Everything could be ordered from Ford with very little fuss.

Today, dealerships tend to use aftermarket sources for spoilers, decal kits, superchargers, alloy wheels, and other must-have accessories to put together special editions.

The two dealer-created special editions we discuss in this chapter are noteworthy because one of them (the Stallion) required a lot of manual labor after delivery to the dealership to create a radically different appearance, and the other (the M-25) is a good example of a local sales team that succeeded where Ford Motor Company failed.

Cars Not Found in this Chapter

Nothing but a newspaper advertisement on microfilm exists of the **1968 California Mod Mustang** coupes created by Shelton Ford in Bethesda, Maryland. The only known features of this special edition are the "vivid vinyl roof" and "unusual accent stripes."

1967 Stallion

Jerry Heasley, one of the co-authors of this book, locates and documents unusual and unique Ford models through his Rare Finds column in *Mustang & Fords* magazine. Stories come from all over the world about Boss 429s that have been turned into dog houses, and Torinos with Police Interceptor packages being driven by 90-year-old church ladies, but in May of 2000 even he was surprised to hear from the owner of a bona fide Stallion.

In 1967, Mainway Ford in Toronto, Canada, advertised the availability of a customized and heavily optioned Mustang fastback exclusively through its dealership. The brochure boasted, "Now in the open and running wild—Stallion—the high-stamina performance car." Literature went on to indicate that the Stallion was "Virile! Aggressive!" which shows those Canadians knew exactly why men bought Mustangs in the first place.

An early standard equipment list included a 390-cid/320-horse (S-code) V-8, four-speed manual transmission, power disc brakes, F70 Wide Oval tires, heavy-duty suspension, limited-slip rear axle, tachometer, styled-steel wheels, woven vinyl bucket seats, console, deluxe seatbelts, radio, deluxe wood steering wheel, exterior decor, interior decor, split deck rear seat, side vinyl trim, and special metallic paint. Extra-cost equipment included an automatic transmission, a 410-horsepower 390 V-8, and a 427-cid V-8—plus anything from the Mustang's famously long options list.

Pictures of a prototype Stallion reveal a head-turning customized rear that incorporated Mercury Cougar taillights into a black panel with the word "Stallion" displayed in large letters above a model-specific gas cap. The "side vinyl trim" referred to a love-it-or-hate-it roof striping treatment that could have been accomplished cheaper and more elegantly with paint. Stallion badging found its way to the front fender and interior, and the light-colored prototype had its non-functional side vents painted black.

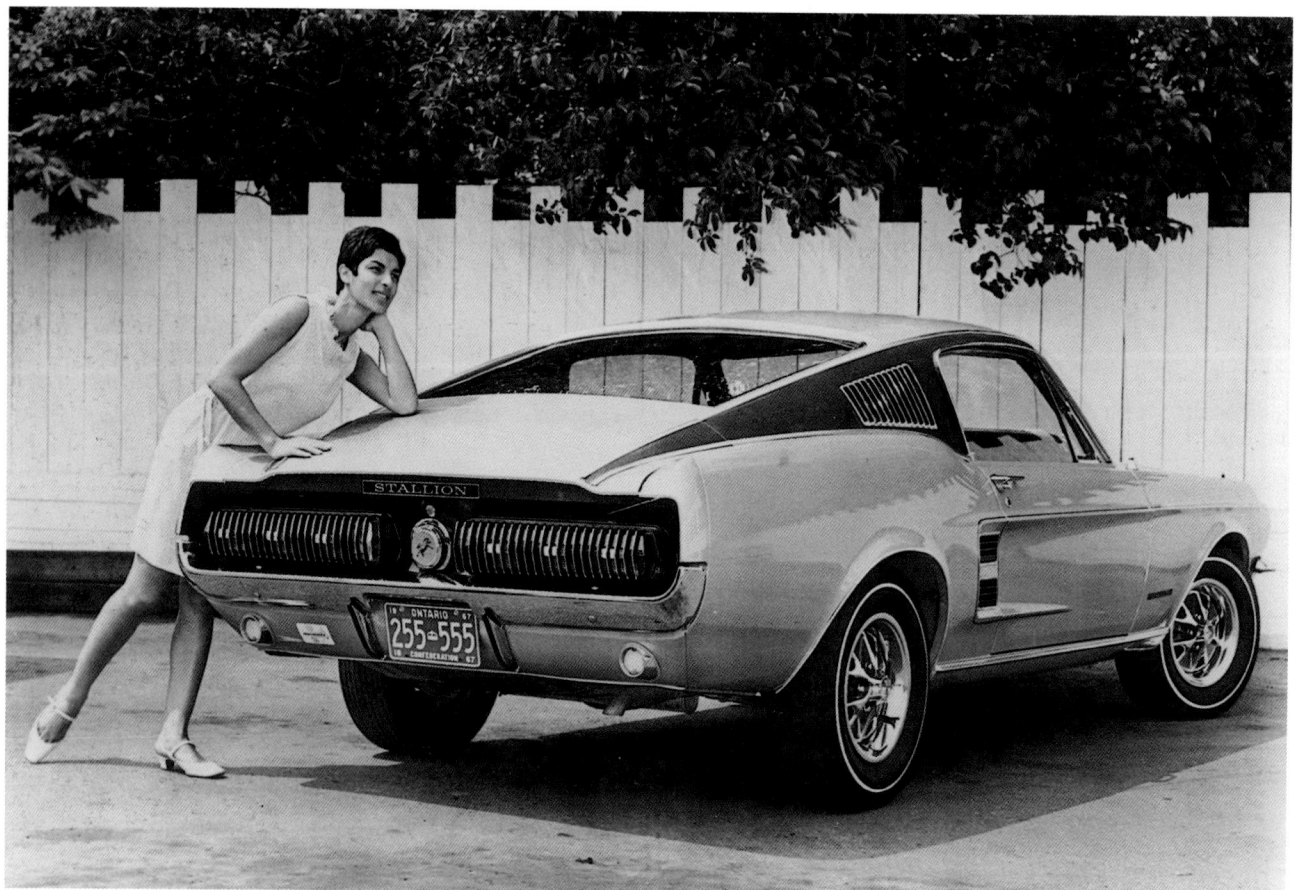

The 1967 Stallion remains something of a mystery to Mustang detectives. *(Joe Faultless)*

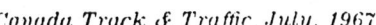

This is the only piece of literature about the Stallion. *(Don Hughmanick)*

Joe Faultless, of Mississauga, Ontario, owns a light-blue metallic Stallion that was modified for racing by one of three previous owners, so its exact condition on leaving Mainway in 1967 can only be guessed at. Faultless' research originally suggested Mainway built 100 of these high-dollar, high-performance Mustangs, but other sources claim production in the single digits. Don Hughmanick's www.limited600mustang.com Web site indicates eight Stallions were made, with four receiving 289-cid K-code V-8s and four getting the big-block 390s.

The name Stallion would be used by Ford in the 1970s on a Mustang II package, and later by Chip Foose for his line of limited-edition designer cars.

THE FACTS

Model Year	1967
How Many Were Made?	between 8 and 100 (est.)
Engines	289-cid V-8 or 390-cid V-8
Reason for Limited Edition	to create a high-profile model for Mainway Ford
What Made It Special?	equipment level, performance package
Registries/Clubs	www.limited600mustang.com

1989 M-25

When it became clear in 1989 that Ford Motor Company would not be producing the 25th anniversary model its Mustang fans requested, one Ford dealership in Overland Park, Kan., used some ingenuity to invent its own.

Before becoming the official "Performance Expert" for Bob Allen Ford, Mike Williams had been formally trained as a commercial artist. Ford blue ran in his blood—Williams' grandfather sold new Model Ts, and his father had owned Osage County Motors in Osage City—and he refused to let the Mustang's 25th anniversary pass without commemoration. No stranger to limited edition dealership specials, Williams had enjoyed some success in the 1970s selling Kansas City performance enthusiasts new Ford Torinos decked out in the popular *Starsky & Hutch* color scheme and Cragar wheels.

Later, he created a hatchback model based on the 1983 5.0-liter V-8 Mustang GLXs with white paint, blue racing stripes, and matching blue interior plus a GT rear wing and hood scoop and mesh-style Carroll Shelby wheels. Following the success of his first faux GT-350, Williams was approved to design more cosmetic packages for his dealership, including a black-and-gold hatchback reminiscent of the Shelby GT-350 Hertz rent-a-racer and a blue-with-silver model.

When it was confirmed in December of 1988 that Ford would not produce its own anniversary model, Williams made several drawings of a 5.0-liter LX-based model from a photo in the '89 Mustang brochure, then designed an appropriate silver graphics package. He liked the rear wing Saleen Autosport was putting on its high-performance models and contacted the company about ordering several for his project. Brad Bowling, Saleen's public relations coordinator at the time, happened to answer Williams' call and talked at length about his as-yet-unnamed special edition.

Each M-25 came with this special plaque on the console. *(Jerry Heasley)*

With its black wheels and Black paint, this M-25 is a Stealth Mustang. *(Jerry Heasley)*

62 • Mustang Special Editions

When Williams asked how to get national publicity for the car, Bowling put him in touch with fellow automotive writer Jerry Heasley, who suggested it be called "M-25" after the fashion of Ferrari's F-40—its 40th anniversary model. A week later, Heasley flew to Overland Park to photograph it for *Mustang Monthly*.

Williams had already completed two M-25 hatchbacks at the time of Heasley's visit—one Oxford White, the other Black—but had plans for a dozen more plus two convertibles. The $1,250 M-25 package included 15x7-inch five-spoke wheels; the Saleen wing; clever side stripes in silver; painted side molding; running horse emblems on the front fenders; M-25 decals; 25th anniversary lettering and decals on the decklid, quarter windows, and backlite; and a serial number identification plaque on the console.

All M-25s were equipped with the popular options of the day—which explains stickers in the $16,000-plus neighborhood—including power locks, dual electric remote mirrors, air conditioning, premium sound system, power windows, sunroof, and rear window defroster. Only the 5.0-liter V-8 was available, but buyers had a choice between the five-speed or automatic transmissions. Automatic cars came with the limited-slip differential and 3.27:1 gears; manuals were fitted with 3.08:1 rear gears.

At present, there is no record of how many M-25s were sold through Bob Allen Ford, but it is known that 209,769 regular Mustangs went to new owners during the 1989 model year, 51.4 percent of which were built with V-8 engines.

All M-25s were ordered with sunroofs. *(Jerry Heasley)*

Mike Williams chose the Saleen rear wing to dress up his LX-based M-25. *(Jerry Heasley)*

THE FACTS

Model Year	1989
How Many Were Made?	n/a
Engine	302-cid V-8
Reason for Limited Edition	to commemorate Mustang's 25th anniversary
What Made It Special?	equipment level, badges, graphics

SECTION 5:

Pretty Colors

The automotive assembly line was a different animal back in 1965.

Back then, guys named Gus touched, lifted, and moved nearly every part of a car so another guy named Gus could weld, paint, poke, and prod those pieces into a complete Mustang.

Today, robots have taken over much of the manual chores in the interest of efficiency. This computerized evolution means the cars coming off the line are nearly identical to each other in every way. Each weld is the exact same length and strength; every paint job is laser accurate to the nearest micron of thickness.

Unfortunately, with perfection came a certain amount of blandness. In 1965 if you wanted to drive a Mustang (or any other car) unlike anything else on the road, it was possible to create a one-off factory paint scheme for a small fee. Virtually any American car could be painted in any color imaginable, especially if that color happened to already exist in the duPont inventory. Like most car companies, Ford was not above pilfering from other makers to please a customer. Columbine Blue, for example, was worn by 1958-69 Dodges as Arctic Blue before it was sprayed on a batch of High Country Specials. That same promotion saw ponies painted Aspen Gold, which came from International, and Timberline Green, which was used on GMC truck interiors a few years earlier. Ford even pirated its own archives over the years; Poppy Red became Flower Power Red in 1969.

Owners of any special order paint Mustangs sometimes have to work diligently to document their unique hues because custom color codes were not included in the VIN nor were they stamped on the data plate or certification label. Body buck tags, which were installed on many Mustangs (but not all), can be helpful in authenticating unusual factory paints, but a build sheet is truly the Rosetta Stone for Mustang detectives.

While it is no longer possible to order one-off factory paint jobs, Ford continues to experiment with limited runs of trendy and unique colors. In today's market, however, a "limited" run usually applies to several thousand units. The two SVT Cobra entries in this chapter take the need for attention-grabbing colors to an extreme.

(Ford)

64 • Mustang Special Editions

One Millionth Anniversary Gold

"What do you do after you build a million Mustangs? Start on the second million!" joked a Ford advertisement in 1966. The company was in an enviable position at the start of the '66 calendar year, and it was during this period that a mysterious, limited run of gold Mustangs was produced and distributed about the United States.

Jim Smart and Jim Haskell have uncovered the only available information about the cars known informally as the One Millionth Anniversary models through their *Mustang Production Guide* and *In Search of Mustangs* database. Both cars in their registry are San Jose-built coupes with assembly dates of March 29, blank paint codes, and a DSO code of 331111.

If each district sales office received one such car, as is speculated, that would place the total number of Anniversary Gold coupes at around 50. The two registry entries have serial numbers only 15 units apart, which suggests the anniversary cars were built as one group and possibly with identical equipment.

THE FACTS

Model Year	1966
How Many Were Made?	50 (est.)
Engines	n/a
Reason for Limited Edition	reward to sales districts
What Made It Special?	unique gold color
Registries/Clubs	www.limited600mustang.com
Books	*Mustang Production Guide, Vol. 2, 1967-73* (1994, Jim Smart and Jim Haskell)

1967 Playboy Pink

photo car owned by Allison Goff

When it comes to car exteriors, pink is one of those polarizing colors—people either love it or hate it. Although it has been known by many creative names—Mountain Laurel, Desert Glow, and Flamingo, to name a few—pink has repeatedly come and gone as a shocking fashion statement since the 1920s.

Because pink naturally receives so much attention, people tend to remember it longer than any other car color, which may explain the lasting myth that Ford produced a limited run of Playboy Playmate Mustang replicas.

When *Playboy* magazine's 1964 Playmate of the Year Donna Michelle received an early Mustang convertible covered in "Playmate Pink" (plus a 21-inch Admiral television, Ventura luggage, 14-carat gold Lady Elgin diamond cocktail ring, and 23-jewel Helen wrist watch), it began a 10-year tradition of similar girlie-colored, four-wheeled gifts from various manufacturers. Despite the fact that several early Mustangs have been discovered with special paint orders that de-code as some shade of pink, Ford did not release the true *Playboy* shade (what one might call "Hugh's hue") until the middle of 1967 production.

Like hundreds of other available special paints, Playboy Pink, as it came to be called, was never promoted nationally as an option. Perhaps Ford did not want to be too closely associated with a men's magazine featuring unclothed women, but several people were aware of Playboy Pink and asked their dealers for it by name.

According to Tony Popish's excellent *Horse of a*

Because Playboy Pink was not part of a package, stock trim was applied unless upgrades were ordered. *(Brad Bowling)*

This six-cylinder 1967 Mustang coupe would be quite unremarkable if not for its Playboy Pink exterior. *(Brad Bowling)*

Although never promoted as a special model by the Ford Motor Company, there was a period in the late '60s when Playboy Pink Mustangs were ordered by dealers to draw attention to their showrooms. *(Brad Bowling)*

Most pink Mustangs from the '60s were repainted a less-feminine color after a few years. Mustang detectives know to look in the trunk and under carpet for a car's true original color. *(Brad Bowling)*

Different Color newsletter and registry, certain Ford dealerships ordered Playboy Pink to draw attention to their lots and showrooms. Marv Tonkin Ford in Portland, Ore., built a whole promotion around 25 pink ponies and a test drive with June 1966 Playmate Kelly Burke. Available records suggest that most Playboy Pink cars were ordered with six-cylinder engines—most likely because they would be driven by "the ladies." But there was one final famous pinkie with serious horsepower when 1969's Playmate of the Year Connie Kreski received a Playboy Pink Shelby GT-500 fastback.

The body tag tells the story on this '67 coupe. "SP PAINT" indicates a special paint order, and MX 707908 tells the Mustang detective this car was originally sprayed with Playboy Pink. *(Brad Bowling)*

Special color cars have a blank space on the data plate paint entry. *(Brad Bowling)*

THE FACTS

Model Year	1967
How Many Were Made?	n/a
Engines	any available Mustang engine
Reason for Limited Edition	glamour halo from first Playmate gift
What Made It Special?	rarity of color
Registries/Clubs	*Horse of a Different Color* 6113 S. Cherry Ct. Littleton, CO 80121

1968 Colors of the Month

photo car owned by Jeff Krueger

Some special edition Mustangs from the past are easy to document because Ford promoted them nationally—the 1968 High Country Special and 1972 Sprint, for example. Others, especially those color-based models of limited run, often disappear off the face of the Earth and leave no trace for modern Mustang detectives.

That would seem to be the case with the "Color of the Month" promotion coordinated by certain Ford dealers in the Denver Sales District in early 1968. Like most special color sales gimmicks, there were no restrictions on body style, engine or option level so there are possibly some amazing combinations still waiting to be discovered in Colorado back yards.

Color of the Month offerings were matched to holidays: Black Hills Gold (New Years), Passionate Pink (St. Valentine's Day), Emerald Green (St. Patrick's Day), and Eastertime Coral (you can probably figure this one out for yourself).

Paint codes on data plates were left blank, as they were on all Mustangs with special colors, but build sheets on Color of the Month cars should reveal the following Ford numbers: Black Hills Gold (WT3822), Passionate Pink

This Passionate Pink coupe was built with the 200-cid inline six-cylinder. *(Jerry Heasley)*

Its Milk of Magnesia hue easily made Passionate Pink the standout of the group. *(Jerry Heasley)*

68 • Mustang Special Editions

Color of the Month specials could be ordered with any trim level. *(Jerry Heasley)*

(WT9036), Emerald Green (WT7819), and Eastertime Coral (WT9012). All Denver area 1968 Mustangs were built at the San Jose plant and should have an "R" for the second character in the VIN. The DSO entry on the data plate will read "51."

There are no numbers currently available to break down how many cars were sold in which colors.

Wire hubcaps really dress up this pink pony. *(Jerry Heasley)*

THE FACTS

Model Year	1968
How Many Were Made?	n/a
Engines	all Mustang powerplants
Reason for Limited Edition	monthly promotion for Denver dealers
What Made It Special?	"exclusive" paint schemes
Registries/Clubs	*Horse of a Different Color*
	6113 S. Cherry Ct.
	Littleton, CO 80121

1968 Colors of the Month • 69

1968-69 Rainbow of Colors

Some of Ford's Rainbow of Colors promotional names—Madagascar Orange, Whipped Cream, Spanish Gold, and Caribbean Coral—sound like drinks you might order at Starbucks. The rest reflect late-1960s psychedelic sensibilities and a love of natural surroundings: Dandelion Yellow, Hot Pink, Forest Green, Sierra Blue, and Moss Green.

According to information uncovered by Tony Popish's *Horse of a Different Color* newsletter/registry, the nine special hues were part of a West Coast push to sell more Mustangs of all body styles in the spring of 1968 and again the following year. All Rainbow of Colors cars were built in San Jose (second character "R" in the VIN) and will indicated delivery to San Jose and Los Angeles sales districts ("72" and "71" on the data plate, respectively). There is reason to suspect the Seattle district (74) participated in the Rainbow of Colors promotion, but no clear documentation supports the theory.

THE FACTS

Model Year	1968-69
How Many Were Made?	n/a
Engines	all available
Reason for Limited Edition	spring promotion for West Coast
What Made It Special?	"exclusive" paint schemes
Registries/Clubs	*Horse of a Different Color* 6113 S. Cherry Ct. Littleton, CO 80121

Grabber 1970

The Grabber promotion was another national color-related spring sales push for Mustangs. Exclusive to the SportsRoof body style, it combined Ford's Grabber colors (Blue, Orange, Green, and Yellow) with certain sporty features to create a "poor man's Boss." Buyers had a choice of two stripe packages: one imitated the 1969 C-stripe minus the Boss lettering, the other was similar to the 1970 stripe design.

Grabber equipment included blackout trim, small "dog dish" hubcaps with wheel trim rings and F-70 whitewall tires. The base engine was Ford's F-code 302-cid V-8 with two-barrel carburetor, but Grabbers could be ordered with either the two-barrel 351 (H code) or four-barrel version (M). Surprisingly, despite the package's low $83 price only 5,120 Grabber Mustangs were ordered in 1970.

THE FACTS

Model Year	1970
How Many Were Made?	5,120
Engines	302-cid V-8 or 351-cid V-8
Reason for Limited Edition	spring promotion
What Made It Special?	equipment level, special paint, decals
Registries/Clubs	www.limited600mustang.com
Books	*Mustang...by the Numbers (1967-1973)* (2000, Kevin Marti)

1996 SVT Cobra Mystic

photo car owned by Monty Seawright

Ford Motor Company held its corporate breath in 1996 when it replaced the Mustang's legendary 5.0-liter pushrod V-8 with an all-new design with single overhead camshafts and 4.6 liters of displacement. The "modular" powerplant had been thoroughly tested in Lincoln products where it won admirers for its quietness and reliability, but Ford was not certain the 4.6 would meet with the approval of hardcore Mustang enthusiasts.

Ford's Special Vehicle Team—assembled to create a new level of performance for the company's popular Mustang, F-150 and eventually Contour—leapfrogged the GT's 215-horsepower SOHC V-8 offering by fitting its Cobra with a 32-valve DOHC 4.6-liter built by specialized teams. SVT's new powerplant, an aluminum-block V-8, produced 305 horsepower at 5800 rpm and 300 lbs.-ft. of torque at 4800 rpm. The block was specially cast by the Teksid company in Italy and shipped to Ford's Romeo, Mich., engine assembly plant where it was fitted with four-valve heads, twin 57mm throttle bodies, an 80mm Mass Air Sensor, and a German-built crankshaft. Twelve two-person teams assembled all 10,000-plus 1996 Cobra motors on the special "Niche Line," then personally autographed a

Cobra gauges have always featured easy-to-read white backgrounds. *(Brad Bowling)*

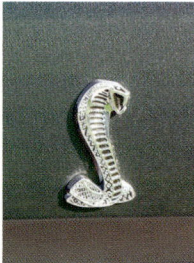
SVT sold 10,006 Cobras in 1996. *(Brad Bowling)*

All 1996 Cobras came with Borg-Warner's T-45 five-speed manual transmission. *(Brad Bowling)*

Depending on the angle and intensity of daylight, the Mystic Cobra can look green, amber, gold, or purple—or a combination of all three. In evening lighting, such as in this photo, the car takes on a solid, dark color. *(Brad Bowling)*

The hood scoops did little more than make the car look sporty. *(Brad Bowling)*

For 1996, the Cobra received its own unique rear bumper cover. *(Brad Bowling)*

The Cobra/Mustang tail lamp housing was new for 1996, incorporating three vertical elements. *(Brad Bowling)*

metallic plate on the passenger-side cam cover. Redline jumped to 6800 rpm, with a fuel shutoff device limited revs to 7000.

The V-code Cobra V-8 was wider and taller than Ford's W-code SOHC model, which required modification to the car's steering geometry, second crossmember, and oil pan. To stiffen the front half of the chassis, SVT installed the firewall-to-tower triangulated brace absent from the 1994-95 Cobras.

Borg-Warner's T-45 five-speed (shared with the GT) was the only transmission available on the Cobra. Rated for 320 lbs.-ft. of torque, the T-45 design made the transmission casing and bell housing one piece for greater rigidity.

Suspension changes involved installing 1995 GT-spec variable-springs measuring 400/505 lbs.-in. in the front and 165/265 in the rear. A larger, 29mm swaybar made for stronger handling in the front, while the previous year's 27mm bar was in place in back.

BFGoodrich T/As were slightly downsized for 1996 Cobras to 245/45ZR-17 front and rear, which saved approximately four pounds of unsprung weight overall. Brake components were unchanged except for the across-the-board upgrade of a new, compact hydraulic unit.

1996 Cobras were fitted with taller, domed hoods sporting simulated air scoops to clear the DOHC engine. The rear valance panel was stamped with "COBRA" lettering, and the rear spoiler became a customer-delete option. Further distinguishing the Cobra from its pony cousin was a coiled snake emblem in the grille and three-inch dual exhaust tips.

The 1996 Cobra interior was a carryover from the previous model. *(Brad Bowling)*

Each of the five openings on the 1996 Cobra's wheel was painted gray. *(Brad Bowling)*

This picture illustrates how distinct the various colors can be with the Mystic paint. *(Brad Bowling)*

This picture shows off the wide DOHC valve covers. *(Brad Bowling)*

The hood was new for 1996. It included twin simulated air scoops and a domed center for more clearance. *(Brad Bowling)*

The 1996 Cobra was the first production vehicle to wear the color-shifting paint. *(Brad Bowling)*

Although the new Cobra was a winner by anybody's estimation, SVT put icing on the cake by creating an unusual, love-it-or-hate-it high-tech color option for 1996. Along with Laser Red, Crystal White, and Black exterior colors, Cobra buyers could order one of 1,999 coupes covered in Mystic paint—a combination of green, amber, gold, and purple colors that showed themselves from different angles, based on the direction and intensity of the sunlight. Controversial though the option was, customers gladly paid the $815 premium to own such an unusual look.

Chemical specialist BASF invented Mystic paint from a process involving color-shifting ChromaFlair interference pigments developed by Flex Products. The principle is identical to what happens when light is split through a glass prism, except that it occurs on a near-microscopic level to produce the changing color effects.

SVT had record sales for 1996 with its Cobra line, with 10,006 of the high-performance Mustangs going to new homes. Of that number, 7,496 were $24,810 coupes and 2,510 were $27,580 convertibles.

There was no special equipment on the Mystic Cobras. *(Brad Bowling)*

THE FACTS

Model Year	1996
How Many Were Made?	1,999
Engine	305-horsepower 4.6-liter DOHC V-8
Reason for Limited Edition	to promote new paint technology
What Made It Special?	expensive, traffic-stopping exterior colors
Registries/Clubs	www.mysticcobra.net
	www.scoa.org
	www.svtcobraclub.com
	www.svt.ford.com
Books	SVT Mustang Cobra Recognition Guide: 1993-2000 (1999, Thomas A Shreiner & Peter C. Sessler)

SVT Cobra Mystichrome

The 2004 SVT Cobra was a carryover of the '03 model—but what a carryover!

Powered by a supercharged 4.6-liter double overhead camshaft engine, the '04 Cobra was in a league of its own. An Eaton Roots-type blower producing eight pounds of pressure sat atop the iron block and boosted output to an advertised 390 horsepower and 390 lbs.-ft. of torque. Reducing the charge heat was a water-to-air intercooler. Aluminum heads saved weight and sped up heat dissipation.

Backing up all that torque was a six-speed Tremec T-56 manual transmission and an accelerator-enhancing 3.55:1 rear axle. The '04 Cobra used a refined version of the independent rear suspension SVT introduced on the '99 model. All Cobras were equipped with driver and passenger air bags, anti-lock braking, and traction control, making them the most powerful *and* safe Mustangs ever.

Aluminum wheels measuring 17x9 inches and 275/40R17 Goodyear Eagle F1 tires sat at the four corners. Brembo's 13-inch vented brake discs and twin-piston calipers were fitted to the front, while the rears were 11.65-inch rotors.

To create an exterior as wild as the Cobra's supercharged performance, SVT once again called on the alchemists at duPont to produce a color-shifting paint similar to the 1996 Mystic option. From its debut at the

The 2004 Cobra was basically a carryover from '03. *(Ford)*

Even the '04 Cobra's leather seats were treated to a dose of Mystichrome. *(Ford)*

The 2004 version of Mystichrome shifts to green, blue, purple, or black, depending on the angle and intensity of light. *(Ford)*

Nothing grabs attention like a 390-horsepower Cobra with color-shifting paint. *(Ford)*

The Mystichrome Package included chromed versions of the Cobra's 17-inch five-spoke wheels. (Ford)

At least two colors are evident in this photo. (Ford)

2003 New York Auto Show, it was clear the Mystichrome Package (code 68M) had accomplished the designers' goal. For only $3,650 above the price of the coupe ($35,370) or convertible ($39,750), a Cobra buyer could drive home in a car that reflected either green, blue, purple, or black, depending on the angle and intensity of light.

ChromaFlair light interference pigments from Flex Products were key to the hue changes, and scientists used a thicker medium to achieve a different result from the '96 application. Carrying the color-shift technology to the extreme, SVT worked with Garden State Tanning (a regular Ford supplier) to create special leather inserts for the Mystichrome Package seats and steering wheel wrap.

The package also included chromed versions of the Cobra's 17-inch rims.

Of the 5,664 Cobras sold in 2004, Mystichrome was applied to 1,010 of them—515 coupes and 495 convertibles.

THE FACTS

Model Year	2004
How Many Were Made?	1,010
Engine	390-horsepower 4.6-liter DOHC V-8
Reason for Limited Edition	to promote new paint technology
What Made It Special?	expensive, traffic-stopping exterior colors
Registries/Clubs	www.mysticcobra.net
	www.scoa.org
	www.svtcobraclub.com
	www.svt.ford.com
Books	*SVT Mustang Cobra Recognition Guide: 1993-2000* (1999, Thomas A Shreiner & Peter C. Sessler)

SECTION 6:

Happy Anniversary!

Everybody loves a birthday, especially automakers, and nothing projects a sense of accomplishment like an anniversary model of a popular car. Such a limited edition vehicle says, "We've been around a long time because we're really good at what we do."

Model years ending in "4" or "9" are usually significant for Ford, which makes anniversaries of five- and 10-year increments all the more memorable. To map this out in a handy chart form:

1964 – The Mustang was introduced.
1969 – A new body style and the Mach 1 were introduced.
1974 – The Mustang II was introduced.
1979 – The Fox Mustang was introduced.
1984 – The SVO was introduced.
1989 – Ford was simply maintaining the momentum of its 5.0-liter sales success.
1994 – The SN-95 platform and all-new body were introduced.
1999 – The New Edge Mustang body was introduced.
2004 – Ford was in the final year of the New Edge design.

Celebrating a fifth anniversary makes a company seem desperate and unsure of itself, so Ford made no fuss over itself in 1969.

Although the 10th anniversary was mentioned in the press in 1974, Ford was trying to establish an identity for its new Mustang II and all but ignored the occasion.

Year 15 came in 1979, as Ford launched its third generation of Mustang along with its "engine of tomorrow" turbocharged four-cylinder, so no mention was made of the anniversary.

In 1984 Ford had several Mustang models to promote, including a new high-tech one from SVO, and the company released a 20th anniversary edition based on the 5.0-liter or 2.3-liter Turbo GT. Naming the model after Carroll Shelby's legendary GT-350 resulted in a lawsuit, but the Oxford White hatchbacks and convertibles with Canyon Red interiors were a huge hit with the public and collectors.

Mustang enthusiasts still talk about the "missing" silver anniversary model from 1989. Celebrating 25 years of production with a special edition seemed like a no-brainer, but Dearborn dropped the ball and never produced one. Keep in mind that Ford was trying to kill off the rear-drive Mustang platform at the time.

By 1994, Ford had remembered the Mustang was its most popular model ever and, while it did not produce a 30th anniversary model per se, the company did bring to market a long-awaited fourth-generation pony.

At the age of 35, the fourth-gen Mustang received some sharp new clothes, more V-8 horsepower, and a special anniversary model.

The Mustang turned 40 gracefully and to much fanfare in 2004. Although the all-new fifth-generation model was still a year away, Ford took the opportunity to send its two-valve 4.6-liter V-8 away in a limited edition version.

The Mustang is now more popular than ever. As this is being written Ford has struggled to meet dealer demand for its 2005 and 2006 cars, which suggests we can look forward to 45th and 50th anniversary Mustangs!

1984 20th Anniversary "GT-350"

photo car owned by Monty Seawright

If a chart were created that mapped Mustang history based on availability of performance models, the period of 1969-70 would represent a sharp peak when no less than eight V-8 powerplants ranging from a two-barrel 302 to a mind-blowing 429 big-block were offered in a confusing variety of Bosses, GTs, Shelbys, and Machs.

A second rise in Mustang performance would show itself very distinctly in 1984, when a performance enthusiast could drive home from a Ford dealership with a grin on his face in one of an array of high-powered machines.

The top step of that ladder was the GT, which came standard with increased power from the M-code 5.0-liter H.O. V-8 with Holley 600-cfm four-barrel carburetor (rated at 175 hp) and a Borg-Warner T-5 five-speed manual transmission. The GT sported a new functional front airdam, signature striped hood, and decals.

As American car makers were building performance into their products again, tire technology accelerated as well, with the Mustang getting the newest shoes as quickly as anyone. GT rubber was upgraded to a 130-mph V-rating for 1984.

Customers who coveted V-8 power with an automatic transmission received a new, F-code 165-horsepower version of the 302 with a throttle body electronic fuel injection (EFI) system and either a three-speed automatic or four-speed unit with overdrive. The V-8 with automatic overdrive transmission came equipped with Ford's new EEC-IV (electronic engine control system, fourth generation), a computer program that monitored engine functions while optimizing performance.

After a disastrous attempt to gain acceptance for turbocharging in 1979-80, Ford improved the reliability and performance of its blown 2.3-liter SOHC four-cylinder (T-code) and introduced electronic fuel-injection to the package for 1983. Featuring an all-new model to highlight

The $1,074 T-roof was a popular option for anniversary model buyers. *(Brad Bowling)*

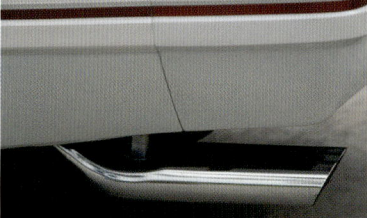

Anniversary cars received stock GT or Turbo GT performance equipment. *(Brad Bowling)*

The 1984 Mustang's T-top system was greatly improved compared to earlier designs. *(Brad Bowling)*

Ford had planned to paint its anniversary Mustangs Polar White, but changed to Oxford White before production. *(Brad Bowling)*

V-8 engines ordered with an automatic transmission were fitted with a new throttle-body fuel-injection system. (Brad Bowling)

Ford applied a burgundy rub strip along the anniversary model's middle. (Brad Bowling)

Anniversary model interiors were Canyon Red with Lear-Siegler articulated sport seats. (Brad Bowling)

the cutting-edge technology, the Turbo GT still failed to draw buyers away from the heavier V-8 offerings (only 3,000 1984 Turbo GT hatchbacks and 600 convertibles were sold), but Ford deserves an "A" for its effort and execution.

Even Ford's workhorse 3-code 3.8-liter V-6 received a throttle-body electronic fuel injection system for 1984, which boosted horsepower to a respectable 120, but the engine was available only with the SelectShift automatic transmission.

Not all of the Mustang line was about performance and speed; standard models were largely unchanged from 1983. The base model was the Mustang L, which included the A-code 2.3-liter overhead cam four with one-barrel carburetor, a four-speed manual transmission, an upshift indicator light to help motorists save fuel, and a starter interlock that prevented drivers with manual transmissions from engaging the car's starter without depressing the clutch pedal. Mustang buyers could get the base L in hatchback form as well as notchback.

Convertible lovers could enjoy droptops in LX form (with standard V-6), as V-8 GTs or Turbo GTs. Throughout the line were new steering wheels with center horn, new instrument panel appliqués and split folding rear seats. Mustang instrument panels had red lighting this year. With the start of the 1984 model year, Ford began producing the convertible on its own assembly line.

Running changes throughout the '84 season can make Mustang-spotting a challenge. For example, some early GTs received leftover '83 hood scoops, but most did not. Integral fog lamps were added to GTs sometime around midyear. In December Ford began fitting Mustangs with its new Quadra-Shock rear suspension system, an arrangement of four shock absorbers that eliminated the traction bars fitted on earlier V-8 cars. Not all changes were implemented—a higher-output version of the four-

barrel V-8 producing 205 horsepower was announced for December arrival but delayed until the 1985 model year (when it would produce 210 hp).

In March and May Ford built 5,260 Mustangs commemorating the pony car's 20th anniversary. Available only on GT and Turbo GT hatchbacks and convertibles, the "1984 Mustang 20th Anniversary Limited Edition" featured an Oxford White (9L) exterior with red "G.T. 350" stripes low on the door, a burgundy rub strip, color-matched grille, and tri-bar running horse logo on the fender. Convertible tops were either white or black.

Interiors were Canyon Red (PD) with Lear-Siegler articulated sport seats and an SVO three-spoke steering wheel (unless ordered with cruise control). Two commemorative panels sit in on the passenger side of the dash—one is a 20th anniversary horseshoe-shaped emblem, and the other is a custom plaque sent to new owners by Ford after they filled out a proof-of-purchase application (but not all cars received this desirable trinket).

The limited edition package (41A) added $427 to the cost of a GT or Turbo GT. Although the VIN does not indicate anniversary status, the metal buck tag attached to the radiator support behind the driver's-side headlight

This Mustang is one of 3,333 GT hatchbacks built in 1984 with the 41A anniversary package. (Brad Bowling)

should read "ANNIV." Of the run, 3,333 cars were GT hatchbacks, 1,213 were GT convertibles, 350 were Turbo GT hatchbacks, 104 were Turbo GT convertibles, 245 were Canadian export models, and 15 were built for executives. The $1,074 T-roof was a popular option with the limited edition hatchbacks.

Standard wheels on the Anniversary cars were base 14-inch, 16-slot cast-aluminum rims wearing 205/70VR14 tires. The TRX suspension package, in its final year, could be had with 220/55VR390 tires and the odd-size forged alloy wheels.

Unfortunately, no one at Ford obtained permission from Carroll Shelby, who owned all rights to the GT-350 name. Shelby, who was working at the time with Mustang "father" Lee Iacocca at Chrysler, sued Ford over the incident.

141,480 Mustangs of all performance levels were produced in 1984.

1984 was the final year Ford offered the odd-size TRX alloy wheels on the Mustang. *(Brad Bowling)*

Ordering cruise control bumped the anniversary edition's standard three-spoke SVO-like steering wheel. *(Brad Bowling)*

It was next to impossible to visit a Ford dealer in 1984 and not realize the Mustang was turning 20! *(Brad Bowling)*

T-top cars came with a vinyl bag to store the panels when not in use. *(Brad Bowling)*

THE FACTS

Model Year	1984
How Many Were Made?	5,260
Engines	2.3-liter Turbo Four or 5.0-liter V-8
Reason for Limited Edition	commemorate 20th anniversary of Mustang
What Made It Special?	specific color, equipment level, graphics, turbo option
Registries/Clubs	20th Anniversary Owners Association PO Box 318 Mount Airy, GA 30563 www.gt350mustang.com www.themustangsource.com
Books	*Fox-Body Mustang Recognition Guide 1979-1993* (2003, Thomas A. Shreiner and Peter C. Sessler) *The Official Mustang 5.0 Technical Reference & Performance Handbook* (2000, Al Kirschenbaum)

Saleen SA-10

1993

photo car owned by John McCauley

Ford's Fox-body Mustang was in its final season of a 15-year run in 1993, seven of which with a nearly identical exterior, interior, and powertrain. At the same time, Saleen Autosport was coming out of an industry-wide recession that had decimated its car sales, and the California-based company was ready to celebrate its first decade of high-performance Mustang production.

During its 10 years in business, Saleen had expanded its Mustang line to several models, each serving a niche in its rabid customer base. For 1993, Saleen offered its entry level coupe ($26,790), bread-and-butter hatchback ($27,490), open-air convertible ($31,690), supercharged SC hatchback ($39,990), and top-of-the-line supercharged SC convertible ($44,490).

Sales were on the increase for 1993 compared with the previous year's abysmal 17 units, and would eventually top out at 102 cars. Early in '93 Steve Saleen announced a limited-edition run of SA-10 anniversary models that would be some of the last Fox-generation Saleens ever made. Production would be limited to 10 copies, and the SA-10s would be available only as hatchbacks featuring a black paint scheme with yellow and white accents to honor

Yellow, black and white were the team colors of Saleen's championship-winning SCCA Showroom Stock cars. *(Brad Bowling)*

These three-piece alloy wheels were standard on all SA-10s and SC models for 1993. *(Brad Bowling)*

Although similar on the outside, no two SA-10s were alike. *(Brad Bowling)*

Saleen created the limited-edition SA-10 to promote its 10th anniversary. *(Brad Bowling)*

Saleen's SCCA Showroom Stock championship-winning race cars. According to company literature, the hatchback body was chosen for commemorative duty as that style would not be returning with the new-for-1994 Mustang design.

Nine people ordered SA-10s, which stickered for $37,995. For their money, customers received a 5.0-liter V-8 with a Vortech centrifugal supercharger and special headers, plus many high-performance pieces first offered on the SSC and SC such as sub-frame connectors, chassis support braces, a rear shock tower brace, and a Panhard rod. Rolling stock was BFGoodrich Comp T/A Z-rated radials (225/45ZR17 on front, 255/40ZR17 on the rear) mounted on three-piece, five-spoke alloy rims (17x8-inchers on front, 17x9s in back). A liberal options list inflated most of the SA-10s past the $40,000 range with interior upgrades, SSC/SC engine parts, chassis stiffeners, and rear axle gear choices. This build-it-yourself policy ensured that no two SA-10s were alike, other than in outward appearance.

In a very unusual marketing move, the cars were available on a first-come/first-served basis to Saleen Owners and Enthusiasts Club members, with the general public gaining access to purchase them once the July 15 deadline was met. Interested parties were asked to submit a refundable $1,000 deposit with their order form. Then-president of the SOEC John McCauley received SA-10 93-0001.

How late in the year did Saleen build the SA-10s? The nine SA-10s wear nearly sequential VINs (the break occurs because car 93-0004 was not ordered) in the 206500 range. Because Saleen did not have its all-new '94 package designed and ready for production there were quite a few "leftover" '93 Mustangs converted—the latest on record being SC 93-0011, which shipped March 13, 1994.

A dash plaque indicates this is the first SA-10 built. (Brad Bowling)

These slanted stripes, which originated with Saleen's 1989 SSC, indicate this is a very special car. (Brad Bowling)

All SA-10s received Vortech superchargers and this vented hood as standard equipment. (Brad Bowling)

This SA-10 featured the $2,200 Saleen leather interior package. (Brad Bowling)

THE FACTS

Model Year	1993
How Many Were Made?	9
Engine	supercharged 5.0-liter V-8 plus owner requests
Reason for Limited Edition	to commemorate Saleen's 10th anniversary
What Made It Special?	equipment level, paint, graphics, engine upgrades
Registries/Clubs	www.saleen.com www.soec.org
Books	The Saleen Book: 20 Years of Saleen Mustangs (2004, Brad Bowling)

Saleen SA-15

photo car owned by Rich Thacker

In 1998 Saleen Inc., the small-volume manufacturer that had collaborated with the EPA on engine upgrades a decade earlier, opened its own in-house certification lab. Because Ford's SOHC V-8 had only managed a weak 215-225 horsepower since its 1996 introduction, Saleen's research and development arm was charged with pumping more ponies out of the 4.6-liter plant.

Saleen was also preparing to celebrate 15 years in the high-performance Mustang business—a bit of timing that inspired the company to create a 10-car run of limited-edition S-281 anniversary specials powered by a more powerful V-8 that would be certified for use in later model years. When Ford announced plans to increase the GT's horsepower to 260 in 1999 through the use of a higher-lift camshaft, coil-on-plug ignition, revised "PI" heads, bigger valves, and a new intake manifold with straighter runners, Saleen chose to forgo certifying the '98 engine and concentrate on improving the '99 configuration.

In the meantime the 10 anniversary cars, known as SA-15s, would be sold with Saleen's Series I Eaton-based supercharger (which was EPA-compliant as an aftermarket product) by way of an emissions loophole that allowed them to be built by the factory but modified by the company's parts department. With 320 horsepower on tap, the SA-15 was the most powerful street-legal 4.6-liter Mustang.

The S-281 SA-15's Speedster body was covered in Ford's Bright Yellow with black markings and a white pinstripe on the vented composite hood. A stand-alone rear

All SA-15s were Speedsters, which included the black light bar and fiberglass tonneau cover. *(Brad Bowling)*

The vented composite hood was standard on the SA-15. *(Brad Bowling)*

Although based on Saleen's S-281 model, the SA-15 wore a rear wing from an S-351. *(Brad Bowling)*

wing set it apart from other S-281s; it was borrowed from Saleen's S-351 model. As Saleen tradition dictated, the cars were built after production of the regular models had ceased for the year—all show shipping dates in December except for 98-0010, which was finished Jan. 15, 1999. Because the company has never produced a car wearing the number 0006, the SA-15 line contains IDs from 98-0001 through 98-0005 and 98-0007 through 98-0011.

During a year when the standard S-281 coupe cost $26,990 and $32,990 in convertible form, the SA-15 had an MSRP of $42,500, and owners were encouraged to raid the options list in order to personalize their purchases. As a result, other than body and wheel color and powerplant, no two were built alike. Seven shipped with the 10-inch rear wheel upgrade; eight had 13-inch front brakes; six were ordered with the 3.55:1 rear axle gears; six had Saleen leather; and there was one automatic transmission in the bunch.

Exterior styling cues were transplanted to the SA-15's interior. (Brad Bowling)

The SA-15 only came in Bright Yellow with matching wheels. (Brad Bowling)

Saleen trimmed its performance pedals in yellow for the SA-15. (Brad Bowling)

Standard S-281s wore this small rear wing. (Brad Bowling)

SA-15s were delivered to their owners at the plant in Irvine as "modified" cars because it was prohibitively expensive to certify the limited run of supercharged 1998 4.6-liter V-8s. (Brad Bowling)

THE FACTS

Model Year	1998
How Many Were Made?	10
Engine	320-horsepower 4.6-liter SOHC V-8
Reason for Limited Edition	to commemorate Saleen's 15th anniversary
What Made It Special?	equipment level, paint, graphics, engine upgrades
Registries/Clubs	www.saleen.com www.soec.org
Books	*The Saleen Book: 20 Years of Saleen Mustangs* (2004, Brad Bowling)

35th Anniversary Mustang

1999

More than any previous birthday, Ford spared no expense in celebrating the Mustang's 35th anniversary in 1999 by sponsoring shows, sending gifts to new owners, and generally reminding everybody why their pony car was by all accounts still America's favorite.

For starters, the '99 model received a much-needed facelift, tummy tuck, and time at the gym. The smooth, almost feminine curves of the 1994-98 design were straightened out and given sharp creases for a more buff appearance. Sides became more vertical and the Mustang gained the tallest rear brake scoop (non-functional, of course) to ever grace a musclecar. A fake recessed scoop on the hood hinted at the air-grabber the Mustang wore in 1968 when it received the first 428-cid V-8. Exhaust tips on the GT model grew from 2.75 to 3.00 inches in diameter. Wraparound headlights took on a sinister glare, while the tail lamps morphed to hard and harsh in keeping with the new look.

The Mustang's new appeal was not limited to its rugged good looks. Under the hood of the GT lay a pumped-up 4.6-liter, still only wearing one overhead camshaft per bank but with 260 horsepower thanks to a higher-lift cam, coil-on-plug ignition, bigger valves, and a revised intake manifold. Even the base model's 3.8-liter V-6 jumped to a respectable 190 horsepower for the occasion.

Invisible refinement lurked in every part of the 1999 Mustang, such as the revised floorpan sealing and foam-packed rocker panels that helped reduce road noise. Subframe connectors all but eliminated the convertible's "mid-car shake," and raising the drive tunnel 1.5 inches gained a small amount of rear suspension travel. Taller Mustangers no doubt appreciated the extra inch of travel built into the driver's seat for 1999. Along with the workout came a strenuous diet, with the pony shedding pounds by switching to sheet-mold compounds in areas such as the decklid.

An optional $230 all-speed Traction Control System (TCS) worked with the Mustang's ABS to reduce rear tire spin in slippery conditions.

All Mustangs—whether equipped with V-6 or V-8 power—received beautiful wreath-design emblems for their front fenders featuring a solid ring encircling the classic running horse and tri-color bar.

Knowing how its loyal fans can't resist a special model, Ford commemorated the birthday of its most popular marque by producing 4,628 copies of a Mustang GT 35th Anniversary Limited Edition in coupe or convertible form.

For $2,695 above the cost of a GT ($20,870 for the

Several of the 35th anniversary car's features would appear again on the 2001 GT. *(Brad Bowling)*

coupe, $24,870 for the convertible), the anniversary edition package (code 54Y) included a special, raised hood scoop (at the end of a wide black stripe); rear deck wing; stand-out side scoops, black honeycomb decklid appliqué; body-color rocker moldings; Midnight Black GT leather interior with silver leather inserts; special floor mats with 35th anniversary script; and special aluminum shift knob (five-speeds only). Exterior colors were limited to Black (code UA), Silver (YN), Crystal White (ZR), and Performance Red (ES). Mustangers did not realize it at the time, but the anniversary package incorporated many of the cosmetic upgrades that would become standard with the 2001 GT model.

According to information compiled by David S. Miller on his Web site www.mustang35th.com, 35th Anniversary production breaks down to 2,318 coupes and 2,310 convertibles. Red was the most popular color (1,555), followed by Black (1,299), Silver (1,259), and White (515).

As if all this weren't enough excitement for the Mustang world to bear, Ford sent every new 1999 owner a 35th Anniversary Courtesy Package that included a letter explaining the gift, an order form for more anniversary merchandise, a commemorative decal, leather keychain fob, leather CD holder, collection of music CDs, Maisto 1/18-scale '99 Mustang replica (in the buyer's color and body style) and a hardback copy of the book *Mustang Chronicle* (written by Jerry Heasley). Someone at Ford must have licked a lot of stamps for that mailing, because 133,637 Mustangs went to new homes in 1999.

Ford wisely introduced the 35th anniversary package alongside its 2000 SVT Cobra R in front of 100,000 rabid fans at Charlotte Motor Speedway in April of 1999. *(Brad Bowling)*

THE FACTS

Model Year	1999
How Many Were Made?	4,628
Engine	4.6-liter V-8
Reason for Limited Edition	commemorate 35th anniversary of Mustang
What Made It Special?	specific colors, equipment level, graphics
Registries/Clubs	www.mustang35th.com
	www.themustangsource.com

Centennial Mustang

1903 must have been a happenin' time in this country. Bicycle repairmen Orville and Wilbur Wright got their homemade bi-wing to float above the North Carolina sand under its own power that year. William S. Harley and Arthur Davidson, working in a 10x15-foot wooden shed in Wisconsin, assembled the first motorcycle to wear the name Harley-Davidson.

For the purpose of this book, perhaps the most significant of the 1903 events occurred when a rural Michigan farmer, racer, and self-taught inventor named Henry Ford produced his first run of Model A runabouts. The vehicles that soon flowed like fire ants from the factories of Ford Motor Company (being the ultimate evolution of the earlier Ford and Malcomson Company and Fordmobile Company) would influence American life unlike anything that had come before. Its Model T, "Flathead" V-8 Model A, F-150, and Mustang would become colorful threads in our social fabric.

In 2003 the Mustang was enjoying a renewed wave of enthusiasm, and its once-numerous competitors/imitators had all become nothing more than footnotes in automotive history books. With the pony car niche all to itself, the Mustang was prepared to serve the young-at-heart market with a range of sporty models.

Base 2003 Mustangs were powered by the 3.8-liter overhead valve V-6 that had been producing 190 horsepower since 1999. Coupe ($18,320) and convertible ($24,020) could be improved with a $345 Interior Upgrade Package that included aluminum finish door lock posts, aluminum shift boot trim ring, stainless steel pedals, leather-wrapped shift knob and four-way head restraints, or a $175 Sport Appearance Group that added a leather-wrapped steering wheel, bright alloy wheels, and a lower body stripe. A $645 Pony Package brought polished aluminum wheels, unique body side stripes, special rear bumper cover, and a leather-wrapped steering wheel.

The GT coupe ($24,305) could be ordered with deluxe or premium trim levels, but the convertible ($29,305) was only available with the premium features.

A Centennial logo was embossed on each of the front bucket seats. *(Ford)*

All 2003 Centennial Mustangs were painted Black (color code UA). *(Ford)*

Two-tone parchment leather was included in the $995 Centennial Package. *(Ford)*

All '03 Mustangs benefited from safer designs for the A-pillar, headliner, and visor. Air bags and safety belts were upgraded to reflect new crash study data, and LATCH anchors were installed for the first time in Mustangs for proper child safety-seat systems.

To commemorate its century of influential automobiles, Ford Motor Company sponsored a gigantic celebration in June where it debuted limited editions of several models, including the F-Series Super Duty truck, Explorer, Taurus, Focus, and Mustang. Because the company's founder is said to have commented about his Model T that customers could have it in any color "as long as that color is black," Ford painted all its Centennial specials black.

All Centennials were fitted with Verona-grain Imola leather two-tone parchment seating surfaces. The 717 Mustang GT coupes and 1,323 GT convertibles were endowed with that line's premium package, which included 17-inch "Bullitt" wheels, anti-lock brakes and traction control; dual exhaust; power driver's seat with power lumbar support; leather-wrapped steering wheel; and Mach 460 AM/FM Stereo with six-disc CD changer, as well as 100th Anniversary badges on the fender and decklid and embossed on the seats. The Centennial Package was a $995 upgrade, and it came with a watch, key chain and leather portfolio cover as part of the Centennial Gift Pack.

THE FACTS

Model Year	2003
How Many Were Made?	2,040
Engine	4.6-liter SOHC V-8
Reason for Limited Edition	100th year of Ford Motor Company
What Made It Special?	paint, equipment level

Cobra 10th Anniversary

photo car owned by Jimmy Morrison

The 2003 Cobra not only met the high standards set by tire-shredding Boss 429s and Super Cobra Jets of the 1960s; it easily surpassed them. Sporting a supercharged 4.6-liter double overhead cam engine, the new Cobra was in a league of its own, with output rated at 390 horsepower and a six-speed manual transmission. With driver and passenger airbags, anti-lock braking on four-wheel discs, traction control, and independent rear suspension all standard equipment, the Cobra was also safer and better handling than its legendary predecessors. As a yardstick of how far the Cobra name had come since the dark days of the 1970s, realize that the 2003 model put out more than three times the horsepower of the 1976-78 Cobra II and King Cobra V-8s and it more than quadrupled the output of the four-cylinder version.

Just when fans of the nearly 40-year-old Mustang thought it couldn't get any better, the folks at SVT announced the introduction of its 10th Anniversary Edition SVT Cobra. It was available in either coupe or convertible body styles with special 17x9-inch argent wheels, red leather seating surfaces, carbon fiber-look interior trim, and unique anniversary badging on the floor mats and decklid. Only 2,003 (get it? 2003) Cobras were built with the 375A anniversary equipment package, which added $1,495 to either the $34,750 coupe or $38,995 convertible. Exterior colors included Black (257 coupes, 394 convertibles), Torch Red (365 coupes, 369 convertibles), and Silver Metallic (381 coupes, 237 convertibles).

The 2003 Cobra's tough-looking, aggressive snout barely concealed an aluminum water-to-air intercooler. *(Brad Bowling)*

SVT has always distinguished its products from standard Mustang models in subtle ways, such as the white-faced gauge cluster. *(Brad Bowling)*

Anniversary Cobras were available in Black, Torch Red, and Silver Metallic. *(Brad Bowling)*

Here's the heart of the beast! For 2003, SVT (literally) boosted the Cobra's horsepower to a claimed 390, but dynamometer reports from some owners suggest an output just north of 400! *(Brad Bowling)*

Twin camshafts have lived under Cobra valve covers since 1996. *(Brad Bowling)*

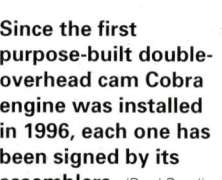

Since the first purpose-built double-overhead cam Cobra engine was installed in 1996, each one has been signed by its assemblers. *(Brad Bowling)*

SVT created its benchmark powerplant by planting an Eaton Roots-type supercharger atop its already strong 4.6-liter DOHC V-8. *(Brad Bowling)*

Don't buy an anniversary Cobra if you don't like red! The interior will sear an image of itself on your retina. *(Brad Bowling)*

No matter which exterior color was ordered, all anniversary Cobras were fitted with the same leather interior: charcoal with red. *(Brad Bowling)*

The anniversary color scheme carried through to the back seat. *(Brad Bowling)*

SVT celebrated its 10th anniversary of Mustang production with 2,003 limited-edition Cobras. *(Ford)*

The only "anniversary" insignia are found on the Cobra's floormats. *(Brad Bowling)*

All 2003 Cobras, whether anniversary editions or not, received TTC T-56 six-speed manual transmissions. *(Brad Bowling)*

Other than the swatch of red around the window and lock switches, this could be any 2003 Mustang. *(Brad Bowling)*

The exterior of the 2003 anniversary Cobra offers no callouts to indicate its special status. *(Brad Bowling)*

THE FACTS

Model Year	2003
How Many Were Made?	2,003
Engine	390-horsepower 4.6-liter DOHC V-8
Reason for Limited Edition	to celebrate modern Cobra's 10th anniversary
What Made It Special?	equipment level, paint, graphics, unique interior and wheels
Registries/Clubs	www.scoa.org www.svtcobraclub.com www.svt.ford.com
Books	*SVT Mustang Cobra Recognition Guide: 1993-2000* (1999, Thomas A Shreiner & Peter C. Sessler)

2003 Saleen SA-20

Any small-volume high-performance automobile manufacturer that reaches its 20th birthday deserves to make a big deal out of the occasion. So many companies have come and gone since the Mustang's introduction (even Carroll Shelby only produced his G.T. series cars for six years before leaving the business) that two decades is indeed a lifetime. In 2003, when Saleen Inc. reached that milestone it created a limited-edition model and threw a party for its exclusive buyers.

Saleen had produced a limited run of top-line Mustangs for its 10th (the SA-10 in 1993) and 15th (the SA-15 in 1998) anniversaries decked out in some combination of yellow, black, and white. Its 2003 SA-20 maintained that tradition, but using a custom-blended pearl white as the base.

Saleen's "standard" car for 2003 was the $36,095 S-281 coupe, which was powered by a 290-horse 4.6-liter SOHC V-8 and modified for performance with the company's aerodynamics package, Racecraft suspension, Pirelli P7000 tires (255/35ZR18 in front, 265/35ZR18 in back), and 18x9-inch wheels. White-faced gauges, performance pedals, a short-throw shifter, leather-wrapped shift knob, and a console plaque announcing the car's individual Saleen identification number freshened up the interior.

For $42,788, a buyer could take home an S-281 S/C that included all of the base model's amenities plus a Lysholm twin-screw supercharger displacing 1.6 liters of air and fuel. This "Series IV" blower was mated to a high-density water-to-air intercooler to produce a healthy 375 horsepower. An SVT Cobra-based Saleen with 390

Saleen's custom pearl white paint gave the SA-20 a distinctive look. *(Saleen)*

The heart of the SA-20 was its 1.6-liter twin-screw supercharger. *(Saleen)*

Center-exit exhaust pipes were optional on other Saleens, but standard on the SA-20. *(Saleen)*

The SA-20 maintained Saleen's tradition of anniversary cars with white, black, and yellow markings. *(Saleen)*

All Saleen Mustangs are individually numbered by the company. This photo car was the first SA-20 built. *(Saleen)*

The simulated light bar and fiberglass rear seat cover were one piece on the SA-20. *(Saleen)*

The new-design SA-20 tonneau cover/light bar became the 2004 Speedster package. *(Saleen)*

The SA-20 came standard with a 375-horsepower 4.6-liter SOHC V-8. *(Saleen)*

The SA-20 shared its twin-vent hood with the S-281 S/C. *(Saleen)*

horsepower could be had for $47,664, but the absolute top of the hierarchy was the 445-horse S-281E that retailed for $60,586 in coupe form and $64,504 as a convertible. The public cast its vote for the middle child, with 57 percent of the 402 Mustangs Saleen built in 2003 going out as S/Cs.

The 10 cars of the SA-20 anniversary series, built on the popular S/C platform, were all convertibles fitted with the S-281E's rear wing, plus anniversary-specific equipment such as a Speedster tonneau cover (with integrated light bar), custom painted pearl white wheels, SA-20 graphics, and ID, console plaque, door panels, floormats, and key fob.

Designer Phil Frank's look for the anniversary model was almost entirely white, with a wide black stripe running from the grille opening to the base of the windshield and a yellow pinstripe separating the two. All 10 cars had black tops.

The $54,357 price (including a $10,000 non-refundable deposit) covered airfare for two to Irvine, one night's lodging, a celebratory dinner with Steve Saleen, and attendance at the facility's seventh annual car show on Sept. 13th, where the model made its debut.

Buyers were encouraged to go nuts with the options, which included anything from the S-281 list. Brake upgrades were the most popular SA-20 extra-cost equipment, followed by the 18x10-inch rear wheel option, Performance Cooling equipment, MaxGrip differentials,

Saleen carried the black, yellow and white colors to the interior. *(Saleen)*

There were special touches everywhere on the SA-20 that distinguished it from the rest of the S-281 line. *(Saleen)*

The leather-covered sport seats fit snugly against the contoured Speedster cover. *(Saleen)*

Saleen began putting white-faced gauges in its Mustangs in 1994. *(Saleen)*

The SA-20 was based on Saleen's popular S-281 S/C model, which featured a Lysholm twin-screw supercharger in addition to the company's other high-performance equipment. *(Brad Bowling)*

and 3.55:1 rear axle gears. Saleen initially built six cars to order for customers, then produced another four for dealers to round out the series.

The anniversary cars were ordered directly through Saleen by way of Villa Ford on North Tustin Avenue in Orange. Delivery to customers either took place at the company's Irvine plant or by enclosed freight shipping (a $1,375 option).

THE FACTS

Model Year	2003
How Many Were Made?	10
Engine	375-horse supercharged 4.6-liter SOHC V-8
Reason for Limited Edition	to commemorate Saleen's 20th anniversary
What Made It Special?	equipment level, paint, graphics, unique interior
Registries/Clubs	www.saleen.com www.soec.org
Books	*The Saleen Book: 20 Years of Saleen Mustangs* (2004, Brad Bowling)

40th Anniversary Mustang

Ford Motor Company was ready to retire the final vestige of its Fox Mustang parts legacy at the end of 2004. Although it had been gradually improving the third-generation pony since its introduction in 1979, the '04 Mustang still harbored traces of the once high-tech Fox DNA deep in its chassis.

Thanks to early teaser photos of an astoundingly beautiful 2005 replacement, the country was suffering from "next-generation" fever and therefore needed some prodding to buy the '04, which was essentially identical to the '01. Mechanically, things stayed the same for 2004—stiffer accessory drive brackets and more refined bearings were the major improvements—with the base model receiving a 3.8-liter, 190-horsepower V-6 and the GT benefiting from a peppy 260-horse 4.6-liter V-8. Both powerplants could be hooked to standard five-speed manual transmissions or four-speed automatics, and all Mustangs wore disc brakes at the front and rear. The V-6 Mustang ranged in price from $18,660 (40/100A base coupe) to $26,520 (44/160A premium convertible); GTs ran anywhere from $24,185 (42/130A deluxe coupe) to $29,695 (45/180A premium convertible).

The only other choices a buyer had to make were exterior color and coupe or convertible body style. Color choices increased by two this year, adding Competition Orange and Screaming Yellow.

Ford had learned from its mistake in 1989 never to ignore the Mustang's birthday, and it came to the party ready to celebrate. For starters, every '04 Mustang wore a special round fender emblem regardless of powerplant or body style. The real present, though, was a 40th Anniversary Package (order number 434) that could be added to either the Premium V-6 coupe/convertible or Premium GT coupe/convertible for $895 extra and included all the equipment in the $345 Interior Upgrade. It was available in Black (color code UA), Oxford White (Z1), or Crimson Red (Z1, the one color exclusive to the package), with Arizona Beige Metallic performance stripes on the hood, decklid and rocker panels. Gold-accented 16-inch wheels were installed on V-6 models ordered with package no. 434, and GTs received the 17-inch American Racing Torq-Thrust rims introduced on the 2001 Bullitt.

All 40th Anniversary interiors were Medium Parchment (color code H) and included a four-way head

This round badge came on every 2004 Mustang. *(Brad Bowling)*

(Brad Bowling)

restraint, painted center console surround and shifter bezel in metallic gray, plus door knobs, shift boot trim ring, and pedals covered in brushed aluminum. Convertibles were fitted with Parchment tops (M code). Commemorative floormats read "Fortieth Anniversary" and displayed the famous running horse emblem; a special metallic plaque at the base of the radio stack indicated the car's owner spent an extra $895 for the limited edition.

Ford built 5,700 of its 40th Anniversary Mustang packages, one of which became an instant collectible when it rolled down the Dearborn assembly line late in 2003 to great fanfare as the 300 millionth vehicle produced by the company since its founding in 1903.

Mustang enthusiasts from around the world celebrated the car's 40th birthday on April 17 during the Mustang Club of America's Grand National show at Nashville Motor Speedway. More than 3,000 Mustangs were on display in 140 classes, 37 of which had been shipped over from Europe as part of an international, seven-week Great American Pony Drive II. Three hundred cars participated at different times in a Mustangs Across America Drive that began in Los Angeles and terminated in Nashville.

The Arizona Beige Metallic stripes were continued on the decklid. *(Brad Bowling)*

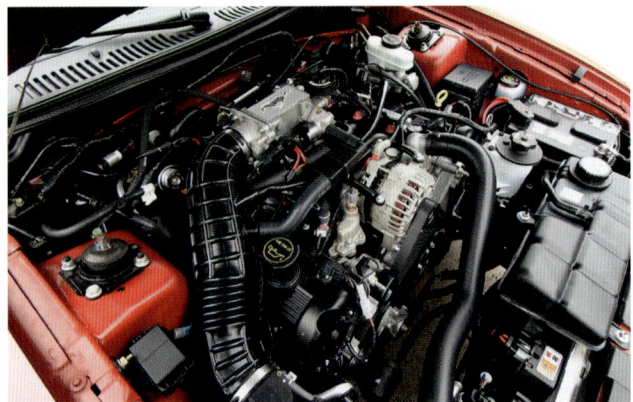

No upgrades were made to the 4.6-liter V-8 engine. *(Brad Bowling)*

Standard Mustang floormats received this embroidered insignia. *(Brad Bowling)*

Arizona Beige Metallic performance stripes were applied to the anniversary cars no matter their exterior color. *(Brad Bowling)*

Crimson Red (code FX) was the only color exclusive to the 40th Anniversary Package. *(Brad Bowling)*

This tiny plaque documents the car's limited edition status. *(Brad Bowling)*

THE FACTS

Model Year	2004
How Many Were Made?	5,700
Engine	3.8-liter V-6, 4.6-liter SOHC V-8
Reason for Limited Edition	to commemorate Mustang's 40th anniversary
What Made It Special?	equipment level, paint schemes

SECTION 7:

Hard-Charging Performance Specials

Much of the book to this point has been devoted to Mustangs produced in limited numbers with special paint jobs, decals, or plaques with state mascots.

We will now spend some time with cars that really get the blood pumping—the hard-charging performance specials that, in their day, represented the best from Ford, Shelby, Saleen, SVT, and Roush.

1965 Shelby GT-350R

Ford was on a tear in the racing world of the 1960s, its engines famously powering Carroll Shelby's lightweight roadsters to one victory after another in the United States and in Europe. Ford knew its popular new Mustang could have the same racing credentials and was prepared to earn them—money no object! How the Mustang and the winning driver of the 1959 LeMans came to be permanently associated is the kind of story Hollywood pays writers good money to invent.

After a heart condition forced Shelby into retirement from racing, he tried to convince Chevrolet to work with him on a series of limited-production roadsters to be powered by the company's small-block V-8. Failing to gain their interest, Shelby knocked on Ford's door in 1962 and convinced Henry Ford II he could combine its 260-cid V-8 with a lightweight British roadster chassis (made by AC) to create a Corvette-beater for the street and track. Ford II had higher aspirations than his competition at General Motors—he wanted Ford drivers to stand on the podiums of Europe currently dominated by Enzo Ferrari's men. Shelby was challenged to create a stable of world class race cars.

Shelby's first roadster prototype, the "260" Cobra, was unveiled at the 1962 New York Auto Show. From that first lightweight racer sprang the faster "289" and fantastically

R-model bumpers were removed to save weight, and this fiberglass apron was installed on the front with improved airflow. *(Jerry Heasley)*

R-model GT-350s appear to sit lower than the street version, but it is an optical illusion created by the wider tires. *(Jerry Heasley)*

The twin Guardsman Blue stripes were originally optional, but most R-models today have them. *(Jerry Heasley)*

This R-model was an original factory racer shipped from Shelby American to Peru. *(Jerry Heasley)*

fast "427" versions. Although only about 1,000 Cobras were made up through the mid-1960s, they were so startling that even now, nearly 40 years later, the Cobra name universally translates as "ultimate, unparalleled performance!"

In 1964, just as Shelby's crew came within six points of catching Ferrari for the World GT Championship, Ford asked him to give its new Mustang the Cobra treatment. The California-based modifier created a pony that could strike like a snake.

The name "Cobra" (legend has it) came to Shelby in a dream, but his high-performance Mustang model was supposedly labeled "GT-350" when Shelby asked how many feet separated his operation's main assembly line from the engine room.

GT-350 production began in December of 1964 when Ford began shipping allotments of Wimbledon White fastbacks directly from its San Jose plant. All Shelby-bound Mustangs were equipped with 289-cid/271-horsepower K-code V-8s and black interiors, but minus many factory parts such as hoods, rear seats, exhaust systems and decorative grille bars.

Running the first year's production of GT-350s all in white was done more for practicality than for the sake of style. In order to operate as efficiently as possible, it was decided to stick to one color so the Ford and Shelby assembly lines could be better coordinated; white was the obvious color choice since it was assumed that many GT-350s would find their way to racetracks and be painted to suit the owner's taste.

Automakers of any size run into supply problems and change vendors in the middle of a model run. Shelby American was no different, and there were several "running changes" made to the GT-350 production line. For example, the 16-inch wood-rimmed, three-spoke steering wheel on

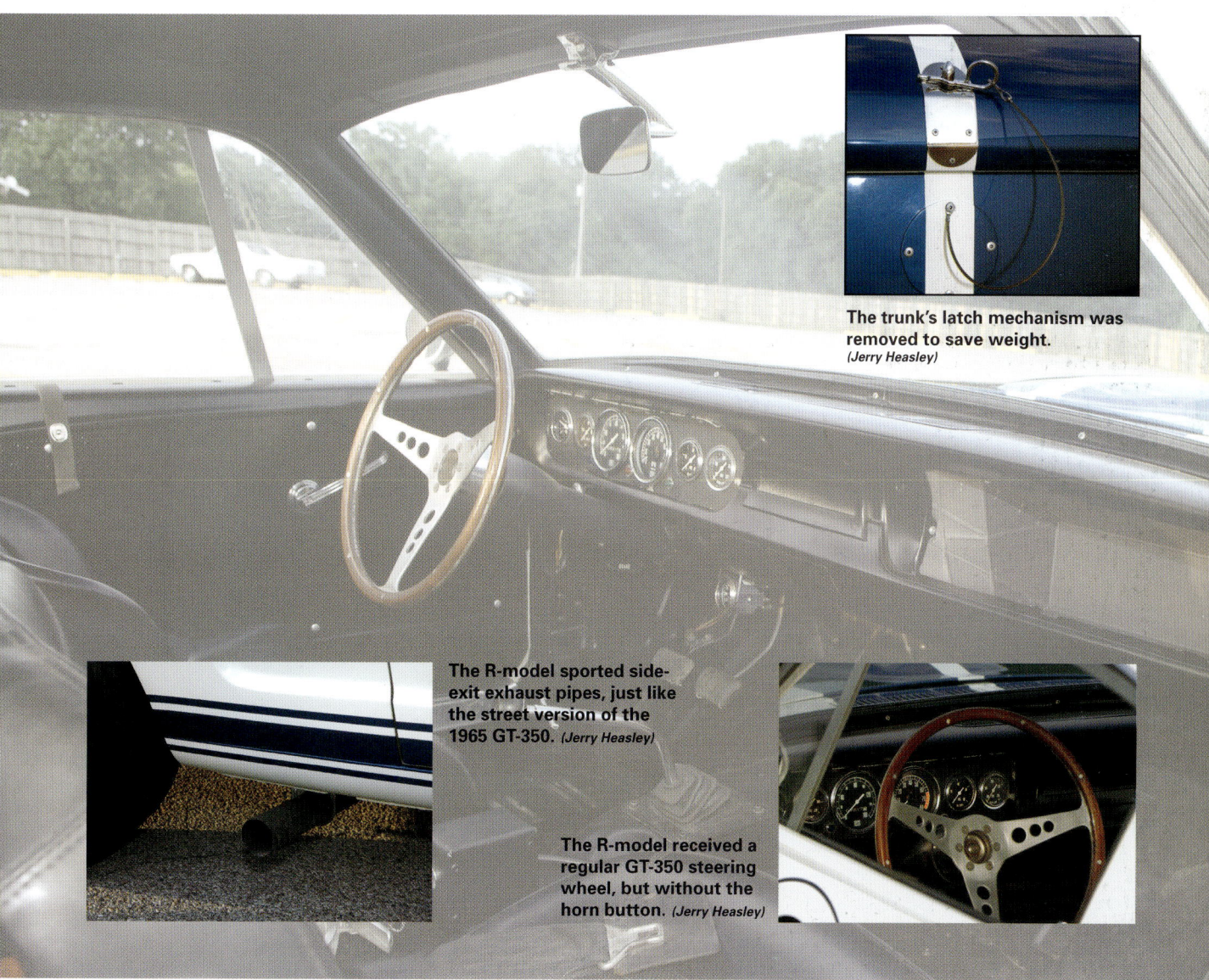

The trunk's latch mechanism was removed to save weight. *(Jerry Heasley)*

The R-model sported side-exit exhaust pipes, just like the street version of the 1965 GT-350. *(Jerry Heasley)*

The R-model received a regular GT-350 steering wheel, but without the horn button. *(Jerry Heasley)*

Shelby claimed its R-model interior could not catch fire because there was practically nothing to burn. *(Jerry Heasley)*

early Shelbys was found to rub against some drivers' thighs and was replaced by a 15-inch unit. Once that change was in place, Shelby's English supplier for the steering wheel (the same craftsmen who produced similar pieces for the Cobra) began randomly changing little style elements from batch to batch. Such running changes were almost never recorded and mattered little to the crew on the production line.

Modifying the Mustang's suspension for GT-350 duty meant adding a thicker front sway bar, longer idler and Pitman arms, lowered upper control arms, over-ride traction bars, and Koni adjustable shock absorbers. Heavy-duty brake pads were added to the stock Mustang system.

Shelby modified the stock K-code V-8 engine with a "Cobra" aluminum high-rise intake manifold, 715-cfm Holley four-barrel carburetor, "Cobra" cast aluminum finned valve covers, a "Cobra" finned cast aluminum 6.5-quart oil pan, steel tubing "Tri-Y" exhaust headers, low-restriction mufflers, and dual side-exit exhaust pipes. Shelby advertised that his modifications resulted in 306 horsepower.

Shelby installed a "Monte Carlo" bar, a strong piece of steel that ran between the two shock towers to prevent chassis flex under hard acceleration or cornering, and relocated the battery to the trunk for better weight distribution. (Victim to another running change, battery relocation ended after some customers complained of smelling acid fumes in the interior.)

A heavy-duty shortened Galaxie rear end with a Detroit Automotive no-spin gear unit and aluminum Borg-Warner T-10 four-speed transmission beefed up the rest of the powertrain. Stock wheels measuring 15x5.5 inches were stamped steel production pieces from Ford's big station wagons, but many customers opted for the Cragar and American Racing rims. As a Goodyear distributor, Shelby was able to give his GT-350s the best street rubber available at the time—Goodyear Blue Dots.

Fiberglass hoods with a built-in, functional scoop saved weight for the GT-350s, although several different

Only the necessary gauges were installed in a custom-made panel. (Jerry Heasley)

versions would be produced during the 1965-66 run as attempts were made to prevent cracking. The hood latch mechanism was deleted altogether, and NASCAR-style pins locked everything down.

A representative of the Sports Car Club of America (SCCA) sanctioning body had told Shelby early on that any Mustang competing in their series would have to be a genuine two-seater—the Mustang's factory fold-down rear seat did not count! To achieve this, the Shelby American crew installed a fiberglass shelf where the stock seat would have been, and a spare tire to take up much of the room.

The GT-350 had a look now legendary—a tri-bar Guardsman Blue paint stripe ran along the rocker panel and door bottom, with a "G.T. 350" logo rendered in 3M tape. Optional twin, 10-inch-wide blue racing "LeMans" stripes that ran from the front to the rear over the top of the car were added by many dealerships.

According to accounts from 1965, the $4,547 GT-350 was the most brutal car ever built for the general public. Like a race car, it was beastly fast and required a heavy foot and strong arms to drive it to its potential. Unlike a race car, it could be purchased at Ford dealerships and came with a full warranty. Shelby sold 526 of the white fastbacks in that first year.

Concurrent with the development of the GT-350 street car, Shelby engineers were working on a GT-350R prototype for the track. To be able to race its R-model in SCCA's 1965 season, Shelby American had to prove production of 100 street GT-350s by January 1. Despite an

The piece of steel tying the shock towers together is a Monte Carlo bar. (Jerry Heasley)

R-models received heavy-duty oil coolers. (Jerry Heasley)

impossible deadline, the company met its homologation requirements with a slight bit of trickery—the crew parked all 110 white fastbacks (the majority of which were still stock Mustangs) from its first Ford shipment in the ready-to-ship lot and pretended they were finished cars when the inspectors visited.

Mustangs destined to become R-models were built in separate batches at the San Jose plant and were shipped to Shelby without interiors, upholstery, headliners, sound-deadening material, side or rear glass, heaters, exhaust systems, and gas tanks. Because SCCA rules allowed modifications to the engine *or* suspension (but not both), Shelby designed his street GT-350 with full-on competition-grade underpinnings. The K-code engines were removed at Shelby American and given a Cobra-style race treatment that included balancing, blueprinting, ported and polished heads, and the installation of single Holley four-barrel carburetors and special "Tri-Y" headers. Once Cobra-ized, R-model motors produced between 325 and 360 horsepower.

Front and rear fenders were flattened, flared, and given new radii to allow fitment of 7x15-inch American Racing magnesium wheels. Bumpers were removed, as per SCCA allowances, and a fiberglass front apron was installed on each R-model for improved airflow to the high-capacity radiator, oil cooler, and disc brakes. The Mustang's stylish rear quarter vents were pulled, the opening covered by a triangle of flat aluminum. Pins not only kept the fiberglass hood down; one also took the place of the trunk latch mechanism.

Other than the windshield, there was no glass on the R-model. Side windows were Plexiglas in extruded aluminum frames, and the backlite was also plastic with a dip in the upper edge that Shelby claimed increased top speed by five miles per hour. Replacing the glass not only improved safety, but shaved 45 pounds off the upper part of the car. R-models were either fitted with a fiberglass contoured racing seat wrapped in black Naugahyde or the Mustang's factory piece. Stock door panels were eliminated by the use of flat aluminum sheets and the vinyl dash pad was removed.

Shelby American fabricated its own 34-gallon gas tank by combining the bottoms of two stock 16-gallon Mustang tanks. The three-inch-wide snap-open filler cap was accessed through the trunk.

The $5,995 GT-350R was introduced to the press at Riverside in January and began shipping to eager customers in April who immediately began winning races all over America. Because of their steep price tag (twice the cost of a stock Mustang), demand was quickly filled and production of the 37 1965 R-models did not finish until the '66 calendar year.

Shelby American's serial numbering system was easy to translate in 1965, and it could be found on a small plaque placed over the Ford VIN on the driver's fender. The information breakdown initially told the owner that he or she had purchased a Shelby (S) Ford (F) Mustang (M) produced in 1965 (5), and that it was the 32nd (032) one to be converted that year. Even this system experienced changes during the production year when Shelby realized that there should be a way to differentiate between the street and race-prepared models. As of car number 032, an "S" or "R" appeared before the three-digit serial number, depending on whether the car was a street or race model. Cars already shipped were left with the old numbering system, although 001, 002, and 003 were retrofitted as they still belonged to Shelby American.

R-models were numbered as part of the street car series, but were identifiable as racers by the "R" in the VIN. *(Jerry Heasley)*

THE FACTS

Model Year	1965
How Many Were Made?	37
Engine	289-cid V-8
Reason for Limited Edition	to homologate for racing
What Made It Special?	more power, lighter chassis, stiffer suspension
Registries/Clubs	www.saac.com
Books	*Shelby American World Registry* (1997, Editor Richard J. Kopec)

1966 Shelby GT-350H

With SCCA B/Production race wins and an enthusiastic public reception in 1965, Carroll Shelby's GT-350 program was renewed for a second year. Ford Motor Company, however, set a higher sales goal for the GT-350s and that meant making a few changes.

Like a lot of conversion companies, Shelby American did its work all year, but Ford shut down every July to prepare for the annual new model changeover. Shelby received 252 1965 fastbacks from the San Jose plant before the end of '65 production and immediately began building them into '66 GT-350s. Those early '66s had Plexiglas inserts in place of the Mustang's rear air vents and a functional rear brake air scoop mounted just rearward of the door, but they were otherwise identical to the run of '65 GT-350s. Once the '66 Mustang grilles were delivered, the batch of cars was completed and shipped.

More changes would come, though, to the remaining '66 run. Executives and efficiency experts had been visiting the Shelby American plant and making their notes since late in 1965. Their comments outlined ways the GT-350 could be made more cheaply and have broader appeal to the Mustang-hungry market. For example, the clunky Detroit Locker rear axle and super-stiff competition suspension were deemed too expensive, costly, time-consuming, and uncomfortable to the average driver to remain standard equipment.

The Ford dealers had spoken—they wanted sporty, but comfortable, cars that could seat four and be serviced by the average dealership mechanic. In short, they were asking for a slightly faster Mustang that did not list for $1,000 more than a loaded Galaxie (as the non-luxurious 1965 had). Color options, automatic transmissions, and rear seats were considered high priorities.

GT-350s with automatic transmissions received smaller four-barrel carburetors. *(Jerry Heasley)*

Cars built late in the '66 run could be ordered with a radio. *(Jerry Heasley)*

The '66 Mustang grille was the only factory piece that affected the appearance of the second-year GT-350. *(Jerry Heasley)*

Other than this owner's personalized license plate, there is no way to distinguish from the rear between a regular GT-350 and a Hertz model. *(Jerry Heasley)*

All accounts indicate Carroll Shelby did not fight the plan to soften his barely disguised race car. The noisy Detroit Locker, in fact, had already been moved to the options list in literature advertising the 1966 model. The first 252 carryover '66 cars had their A-arms lowered as per '65 specs, but most GT-350s that followed would retain the stock Ford geometry. Race-ready traction override bars were replaced by cheaper, easier-to-install units, and Koni's adjustable shock absorbers were gradually phased out. Back seats became standard equipment (the '65 shelf was optional in '66), and the imported wood steering wheels were replaced with stock Mustang GT pieces with GT-350 logos. The tri-bar lower body striping would be a complete 3M tape product for remaining '66 cars.

Dealers and the public were happy to see that these changes produced a substantial price drop to $4,428. Other buyer-friendly amenities included paint options such as Candyapple Red, Sapphire Blue, Ivy Green, Wimbledon White, and Raven Black. GT-350 owners could putt around town with an optional C-4 high-performance automatic transmission (which brought a 595-cfm carb), and an AM radio joined the list midyear.

Toward the end of the '66 run Shelby offered a Paxton supercharger option for $670, claiming it would produce up to 46 percent more power from the K-code 289 V-8. The warranty for blown GT-350s covered a short 90 days or 4,000 miles; only 11 were ordered with the Paxton.

Just as Ford and Shelby had predicted, there was a substantial increase in GT-350 sales in 1966—a total of 2,378 cars. Forty percent of that figure came from a contract Shelby got to build his fastbacks for the Hertz Sports Car Club. A special run of 1001 GT-350H fastbacks was put into service as rental cars—mostly in black-with-gold paint schemes, but later in all 1966 Shelby colors. Early H-models were part of the 1965 carryover line and included all of the heavy-duty suspension modifications. Hertz later asked that all of its

Contrary to popular belief, not all GT-350H models were black with gold stripes. *(Jerry Heasley)*

Only the early '66 GT-350s had their A-arms lowered; later ones retained the stock Ford suspension geometry. *(Jerry Heasley)*

All '66 Shelby Mustangs received Plexiglas rear quarter windows. *(Jerry Heasley)*

GT-350s come with automatic transmissions and a brake booster for the stiff competition-style brakes.

Receiving the Hertz order was a pivotal factor in Shelby production. Guaranteeing nearly 1,000 cars (the original pitch to Hertz executives was for 100 units) put Shelby American in a better position to bargain with its suppliers. The sale also meant that the average traveler could be exposed to the GT-350, a point that no doubt increased non-Hertz sales for 1966 and later. Featuring the GT-350 in all of Hertz' national advertising didn't hurt, either.

The GT-350H began and ended with the 1966 model year, but Shelby would sell regular production cars without special graphics or paint schemes to Hertz in 1968 and '69.

All GT-350H cars received black interiors. *(Jerry Heasley)*

THE FACTS

Model Year	1966
How Many Were Made?	1,001
Engine	289-cid V-8
Reason for Limited Edition	contract with Hertz rental car agency
What Made It Special?	colors, non-factory equipment
Registries/Clubs	www.saac.com
Books	*Shelby American World Registry* (1997, Editor Richard J. Kopec)

Mustang II King Cobra

photo car owned by Monty Seawright (King Cobra)
photo car owned by Lou McCoy (Cobra II)

The 1974-78 Mustang II series is arguably the most controversial generation in the Mustang's 40-year history, but most enthusiasts are willing to concede a model or two with a spark of excitement.

To be truthful, in hindsight the downsized II platform did one thing very well; it kept the Mustang name alive at a time when other bloated marques were dying off. Gorging itself on market success, Ford allowed the once-fit pony car to balloon in size and weight until by 1973 it was as heavy as some mid-size family sedans. With input from marketing clinics and thousands of vocal fans, Ford designed a smaller vehicle with styling cues from the original and a somewhat modern four-cylinder engine for better economy. Many factors were taken into account during the creation process—government-imposed emissions restrictions, rising insurance premiums for performance cars, and a market that suddenly seemed smitten by small, sporty cars from Japan and Germany were three of the most dominant.

Gone forever were big-block V-8 engines from the Mustang's option list; in fact, there were no V-8s offered in the 1974 model year. Only two powerplants were available for '74—the base 2.3-liter "Lima" four-cylinder with a single overhead camshaft and an optional 2.8-liter V-6 from Ford of Germany's Mercury Capri. The two body styles—a two-door coupe and three-door hatchback—each measured 11.8 inches less than the '73 they replaced.

Although it has often been derisively called the "Pinto Mustang," the '74 shared fewer parts with its cheaper Ford cousin than people realize. Ford wanted a big-car luxury ride in its small package, so interior noise was greatly reduced by melting rubber sheets into the floorpan during assembly. Powertrain noises were addressed by the use of a larger-diameter driveshaft. A U-shaped, isolated subframe (known to Ford engineers as the "toilet seat")

Excessive pinstriping in contrasting colors was a hallmark of American performance cars from the late 1970s. *(Brad Bowling)*

Not exactly subtle, the King Cobra's graphics made it clear this was a special Mustang. *(Brad Bowling)*

None of the Mustang IIs, even the King Cobra, had reclining front seats. *(Brad Bowling)*

T-top Mustang IIs came with a vinyl bag and rear tie-downs to store the removeable panels. *(Brad Bowling)*

killed much road noise before it could get to the passenger compartment. The new suspension was independent in the front and a Hotchkiss-type in the rear.

The look of the Mustang II would remain, for better or worse, unchanged throughout its five-year run. Body design details included separate FORD block letters above the grille, facing upward; single round headlamps recessed into squarish housings; a front bumper that protruded forward in the center, matching the width of the grille; rub strips wrapped only slightly onto the bumper sides; door sheetmetal with a sculptured, depressed area that began near the back and extended for a short distance on the quarter panel, following the contour of the wheel opening; a curvaceous bodyside crease that ran below the door handle; B-pillars and conventional quarter windows on notchbacks; sharply tapered quarter windows that came to a point at the rear on hatchbacks; European-style tail lamps consisting of three side-by-side sections with a small backup lens at the bottom of each center section and larger amber turn signal lenses; large FORD block letters on the panel between the tail lamps above the license plate housing; one-piece fiberglass-reinforced front ends and color-keyed urethane-coated bumpers; wheel lip moldings; side marker lights with die-cast bezels; recessed door handles; and slim high-luster exterior trim moldings.

Bridging the gap between old and new were some features considered essential to the Mustang package, such as a floor-mounted shifter, low-back bucket seats, vinyl upholstery, and full carpeting. Separating the first-generation from the II were such standard niceties as solid-state ignition, front disc brakes, a tachometer, steel-belted whitewalls and—in the 2+2 hatchback models—a folding rear seat.

"Hot" Mustang II models included the Rallye and Mach 1, both of which were equipped with the 2.8-liter V-6 engine. The Rallye came with a limited-slip differential; raised white-letter steel-belted tires; an extra-cooling package; a competition suspension; dual color-keyed; remote-control door mirrors; styled steel wheels; a Sport exhaust system; a digital clock; and a leather-wrapped steering wheel.

Base prices that first year ran from $3,081 to $3,621 for the Mach 1 package, but showroom stickers initially crossed the $4,500 mark because of long options lists. With some adjustments by the factory, prices quickly lowered and the new Mustang experienced the line's highest sales records in nearly a decade—385,993 cars (or 4.75 percent of the industry's total output) compared to the 134,817 Ford sold of the '73 model. Although promoted as a sporty or

It is clear from this picture that Ford did not spend a lot of effort or money on the appearance of its Mustang engine compartments in the 1970s. Even this low-mileage example of its highest-profile model—the King Cobra—does not look inspiring under the hood. *(Brad Bowling)*

A front air dam and wheel opening spats distinguished the King Cobra from its less-expensive siblings. *(Brad Bowling)*

luxury vehicle, the Mustang II's real audience was looking for a low base price and economy of operation, which explains why 252,470 of the first-year sales were for the base hardtop and 2+2.

Giving in to market pressure, Ford made some structural modifications to the Mustang II for 1975 to make way for a 5.0-liter V-8 engine. Wearing primitive smog controls and struggling with unleaded gasoline, the '75 Mustang II's 302-cid powerplant was a distant cousin to the Boss engine of the same size. Output ranged from 122 to 139 horsepower during its four years in the II series, but the V-8 could be had in coupe or hatchback models at a time when most car companies were phasing out anything larger than a V-6.

In 1976 Ford gave the Mustang an appearance package to match the performance potential of the 5.0-liter: the Cobra II package—a hatchback-only option with the "show," but not the "go," of a Shelby Mustang. "Cobra strikes again," said the *Free Wheelin'* catalog, a youth-oriented, 24-page color booklet produced by Ford. "New Cobra II. Ford's Mustang II wrapped in an appearance package that does justice to the Cobra name. So striking, it's already a sales success." It was hard to believe from a piece of literature printed in October 1975, that the exciting-looking Cobra option was "already a sales success;" however, the Cobra II was on its way to reaching an approving audience, since the package was available on all 2+2s with any engine.

For $325, a Mustang II buyer could order a hatchback with any of the three powerplants and have it decked out with bold racing stripes; a blacked-out grille; racing mirrors; rear quarter window louvers; a front air dam; a non-functional hood scoop; a rear deck lid spoiler; a brushed aluminum instrument panel and door panel appliques; Cobra insignias on the front fenders; styled steel wheels and BR70 steel-belted tires with raised white letters. The 1976 Cobra II came in white with blue stripes, blue with white stripes, or black with gold stripes

The Cobra II marked the first time since the Boss 429 and Shelbys that Ford shipped a Mustang away for final assembly. Jim Wangers, who is often credited with the success of Pontiac's original GTO, designed and installed the '76 Cobra II graphics and aerodynamic pieces at his small Motortown plant near Ford's Dearborn factory. As a nod to Mustang history, Carroll Shelby even appeared in the sales catalog to promote the Cobra II.

So popular was the Cobra II package that Ford moved its production in-house at the start of the 1977 model year, but otherwise left it unchanged.

The Mustang II entered its final model year in October of 1977 as supreme ruler of the crowded domestic sporty subcompact class, even though there were very few improvements or changes to the basic product. New graphics for the Cobra II would have been the extent of Mustang II news had it not been for the release of a truly over-the-top limited edition performance package – the King Cobra.

Advertised as the "Boss of the Mustang stable," the King Cobra (or "KC") was built around a 2+2 body with 5.0-liter engine, standard four-speed manual transmission, power brakes and power steering. The $1,253 KC treatment

Although the Cobra II design (1976 version shown) was no doubt the basis for the '78 King Cobra, there are several cosmetic differences. *(Brad Bowling)*

The Cobra II package was patterned after the Shelby GT-350 and GT-500 models of the 1960s. *(Brad Bowling)*

did without the customary bodyside striping of the Cobra II/GT-350, but sported a unique tape layout including a giant snake decal on the hood and pinstriping on the greenhouse, decklid, wheel lips, rocker panels, belt, over-the-roof area, and around the side windows. Up front was a tough-looking airdam. A "King Cobra" nameplate went on each door and the back spoiler and a "5.0L" badge appeared on the rear-facing hood scoop. The King Cobra also had rear quarter flares, a black grille and moldings, and color-keyed dual sport mirrors. Raised-white-letter tires rode lacy-spoke aluminum wheels with twin rings and a Cobra symbol on the hubs.

To make the KC a complete "look at me" special, many buyers paid the extra $587 for the T-top option, bringing the sticker price to $5,638 before any other accessories were ordered. Simply adding the $225 automatic transmission put the KC at the $6K mark with tag, taxes and title figured in. Despite its high purchase price, enthusiasts recognized the KC as one of the only Mustang IIs with collector potential and snapped up 4,318 of them.

The 1976-77 Cobra II included Shelby-style thin-thick-thin side striping. *(Brad Bowling)*

The Cobra II's airdam was much smaller than the spoiler found on the King Cobra. *(Brad Bowling)*

While the King Cobra had blacked-out features such as headlight surrounds and grille, the Cobra II retained the chrome look. *(Brad Bowling)*

THE FACTS

Model Year	1978
How Many Were Made?	4,318
Engine	139-horsepower 5.0-liter V-8
Reason for Limited Edition	final year of Mustang II series
What Made It Special?	graphics, equipment level
Registries/Clubs	www.mustangii.net

SVO Comp Prep

1984-86

Ford took its turbocharged four-cylinder concept to a new level in fall of 1983 when it introduced the SVO Mustang. The brainchild of Ford's Special Vehicle Operations department (formed in 1981 to oversee Ford's renewed involvement in motorsports), the SVO Mustang raised the bar on engine technology with its fuel-injected 2.3-liter turbocharged four-cylinder powerplant (code T) and air-to-air intercooler that produced 175 horsepower with plenty of grunt at the bottom of the tachometer.

This very valiant attempt to bring European sophistication to the Mustang herd included a Borg-Warner T-5 five-speed manual gearbox with Hurst linkage, four-wheel disc brakes with five-lug rotors, performance suspension with adjustable Koni gas-filled shocks, P225/50VR-16 Goodyear NCT tires on cast aluminum 16x7-inch wheels, and a functional hood scoop.

According to Ford's published (and much advertised) figures, SVO's Mustang could reach 134 miles per hour and get to 60 from zero in just 7.5 seconds. SVO's shock absorbers and struts had three settings: cross-country (for front and rear); GT (front only); and competition (front and rear). Four-wheel disc brakes were standard.

Sunroofs were popular options during all three years of SVO production. They were not available, however, on the Comp Prep package. *(Brad Bowling)*

Although leather was a $189 option on 1985 SVOs, very few were built with the standard cloth seats. Comp Prep cars were shipped with the cloth seats. *(Brad Bowling)*

This "sail" panel was an SVO-exclusive part. *(Brad Bowling)*

The SVO Mustang was the epitome of high-tech performance when introduced in 1984. *(Brad Bowling)*

The SVO's rub strip changed from black to gray in 1985. *(Brad Bowling)*

This early '85 displays the dual-tip single exhaust system. *(Brad Bowling)*

This shot shows how far recessed the 1984 through early 1985 headlights really were. *(Brad Bowling)*

More than just a Mustang with some techno-toys, the SVO looked different as well. The face was grille-less, with a single slot below the hood panel and a Ford oval sitting square in the middle. Large rectangular headlamps were deeply recessed on the 1984 model, flanked by large, wraparound lenses and supported at night by integrated foglamps. The most striking feature of the new model was its polycarbonate, dual-wing rear spoiler designed to increase downforce on the car at speed. Other aerodynamic aids included rear-wheel "spats" to direct airflow around the open wheel wells.

The SVO was only available in hatchback form, and none were offered to the general public with the Mustang's popular T-roof option to retain the chassis' stiffness (although a few executive-ordered T-top SVOs have been documented). Exterior color choices included Black (1C), Silver Metallic (1E), Dark Charcoal Metallic (9W), or Red Metallic (2A). Interiors were all Charcoal—cloth or optional leather—and benefited from multi-adjustable articulated bucket seats. Standard SVO equipment included an 8000-rpm tachometer, quick-ratio power steering, Traction-Lok rear axle with 3.45:1 gears, leather-wrapped steering wheel, shift knob, and brake handle, unique instrument panel appliqués, narrow body side moldings and unique C-pillar, and tail lamp treatments. A premium/regular fuel switch calibrated the ignition instantly between nine pounds of boost and 15. Pedal positioning allowed "heel and toe" shifting, and a "dead pedal" for the left foot improved the driver's position during hard cornering. Only six major options were available for SVO: air conditioning, power windows, power door locks, cassette player, flip-up sunroof, and leather seat trim.

Early SVOs were built with the Mustang's "slapper bar" system for controlling the rear axle during acceleration; later 1984s were upgraded to the four-shock setup. SVO switched to Goodyear's VR50 "Gatorback" design around the same time.

The only thing preventing the new pony from becoming a runaway big hit was its window sticker; at $15,596, the SVO price tag was twice as much as a base '84 Mustang four-cylinder ($6,885) and $5,834 more than a GT hatchback ($9,762). Magazines and a few performance enthusiasts loved the car—*Motor Trend* called it "the best-driving street Mustang the factory has ever produced." *Road & Track* claimed the SVO "outruns the Datsun 280ZX, outhandles the Ferrari 308 and Porsche 944." High prices, lack of easy availability (Ford dealers were reluctant to order such an innovative car without a ready buyer) and a late introduction kept SVO from missing its first-year goal of 10,000 sales; 4,507 of the turbocharged ponies found new homes in '84.

SVO announced an interesting "Competition Preparation Option" (41C) in April of 1984 for aspiring road

A 2.3-liter SOHC fuel-injected turbocharged four-cylinder powered the SVO during its three-year run. The air conditioner compressor would prove this particular SVO is not a Comp Prep car. *(Brad Bowling)*

The unusually shaped SVO hood required adding an extension to the regular Mustang's latch. *(Brad Bowling)*

The SVO tail lamps had horizontal black lines in the lenses to distinguish them from standard Mustang lights. *(Jerry Heasley)*

Under the hood, the Comp Prep model is identical to the regular SVO, except for the missing air conditioning equipment. *(Jerry Heasley)*

racers and autocrossers. Comp Prep SVOs were shipped to dealers minus the stereo, antenna, air conditioning system, power hatch release, and power locks and windows for a weight savings of roughly 140 pounds. Foglamps were shipped uninstalled with the '84 CP cars; some dealers mounted them before selling, others left them off. Such a setup would appeal mostly to Mustangers looking for a club or weekend racer who would likely remove additional speed impediments such as the back seat and spare tire. Ordering Comp Prep also dropped the window sticker by $1,451. Reported production of 41C SVOs in '84 totaled three cars, but the actual number might have been higher.

Changes to the 1985 model were few. The rear axle ratio was changed to 3.73:1 and the five-speed transmission gears were modified. Suspension upgrades provided a stiffer, better handling setup. Exterior colors were increased to seven: Black (code 1C), Silver Metallic (1E), Medium Canyon Red Metallic (2A), Jalapena Red (2R), Dark Sage (4E), Oxford White (9L), and Medium Gray Metallic (1D). The exterior trim color changed from black to gray.

SVOs built after June 6, 1985, have been labeled "1985.5" models by enthusiasts, and they are substantially different from cars built early in the year. Flush-mounted headlamps were the most obvious visual cue to the car's mid-year status, but it was under the scooped hood where the SVO showed the most improvement. A higher-performance camshaft, higher-flow exhaust system, reconfigured turbocharger, larger fuel injectors and greater boost increased horsepower to 205. The twin exhaust tips no longer exited next to each other, but were separated by the width of the car after splitting behind the catalytic converter.

Because the SVO could be ordered with and without certain options, it can be difficult at times to tell the difference between a "stripper" model and one built as a Comp Prep package. It has been reported that some dealers installed radios in Comp Preps in an effort to move the slow-selling cars. The only way to resolve such controversy is by looking at the Certification Label inside the driver's doorjamb; because different springs were used to compensate for the weight loss in Comp Prep cars, the codes are different. CP cars built in 1984 have the code "HHRR," early 1985s read "GGMM," late 1985s indicate "GGNN," and all 1986 CPs read "GGRR."

Despite this power increase and a generous price decrease (to $14,521), sales fell to 1,951 units—439 of which were 1985.5 models. SVO sold 40 Comp Prep

1984-86 SVO Comp Prep • 111

This 1985-1/2 SVO Mustang was ordered with the 41C Comp Prep package. *(Jerry Heasley)*

These 16-inch alloy wheels were fitted to every SVO built. *(Jerry Heasley)*

From this angle, it is impossible to tell that this SVO has the Comp Prep delete package. *(Jerry Heasley)*

packages for all of the '85 model run, 11 of which qualify as 85.5 models.

The SVO's power rating dropped from 205 to 200 for 1986, its final year of production, due to a more conservative programming of its EEC-IV. The SVO's appearance was essentially the same as in the previous year. Ford boosted its anti-corrosion warranty, added sound-deadening material and adopted a single-key lock system. A third, high-mounted brake lamp was a new safety feature made mandatory for 1986, and the SVO integrated the light into its rear spoiler. Buyers had the option of deleting the bi-plane rear wing and replacing it with the Mustang GT unit. SVO sold 80 Comp Prep packages in '86.

SVO added Dark Shadow Blue (7B) to the color list and changed Medium Charcoal Metallic (1B) to Medium Gray Metallic (1D). The price of the 1986 model crept up to $15,272, and SVO finished the series with 3,379 sales. In all, there were 9,837 SVO Mustangs produced.

Many Comp Prep SVOs became weekend racers. *(Jerry Heasley)*

THE FACTS

Model Year	1985-86
How Many Were Made?	(1984, est.) 3
	(1985) 40
	(1986) 80
Engine	2.3-liter turbocharged four-cylinder
Reason for Limited Edition	to provide a competition-ready model
What Made It Special?	140 pounds lighter (deleted power windows/locks, a/c and radio)
Registries/Clubs	www.mustangsvo.org
	www.svoca.com
Books	*Mustang SVO: The Machine Speaks For Itself* (David LaRocque)
	Fox-Body Mustang Recognition Guide 1979-1993 (2003, Thomas A Shreiner & Peter C. Sessler)

Saleen SSC

photo cars owned by Mark LaMaskin and Monty Seawright

In 1984 Steve Saleen entered the Mustang specialty market abandoned by Carroll Shelby in 1970 and formed a relationship with Ford Motor Company that allowed him to modify its cars right off the assembly line for better performance. Because Saleen only changed certain aerodynamic, suspension, brake, interior, and stereo components in the cars that bore his name and left the powertrains untouched, Ford also fully honored the vehicles' warranties.

In 1988 Saleen was enjoying the fourth straight year of rising sales for his line of high-performance Mustangs. His SCCA Showroom Stock race team had brought home the championship trophy in 1987 and pulled off an amazing 1-2-3 finish at the 1988 24-hour Mosport, Canada, race. The small-volume auto manufacturer was ready for a new challenge.

Ford had no short-term plans to replace the aging Fox chassis or even perform a superficial restyling for several years, which meant Saleen's Mustang would get stale if he did not expand the model line to include engine modifications. Having grown up in Southern California, the nation's poster child for automobile emissions standards,

The standard Saleen hatchback (shown here) for 1989 cost $23,500; the SSC retailed for $36,500. *(Brad Bowling)*

Although most of the SSCs body pieces were standard Saleen items, they looked different on the all-white car. *(Brad Bowling)*

Saleen's SSC had a striking appearance that set it apart from other Mustangs. *(Brad Bowling)*

The SSC marked the first time for a production Fox-body Mustang to wear a non-black beltline rub strip. *(Brad Bowling)*

These stripes originated with the SSC and would continue in one form or another on various Saleen models for more than a decade. *(Brad Bowling)*

By 1989 this wing had become a recognizable part of the Saleen heritage. *(Brad Bowling)*

Saleen knew it would not be easy to build an engine that met federal guidelines for tailpipe output, fuel economy, and reliability. With his SCCA race team shop square in the middle of the Detroit auto scene, however, his idea for a "super Mustang" was at least worth considering.

There was no precedent in 1988 for certifying a powerplant in such limited numbers, nor was there a guarantee the invested time, money, and effort would have a payoff. The Environmental Protection Agency was still in the process of sorting out guidelines for working with the automotive aftermarket. Saleen hired Terry Hudyma, a former EPA employee, who was in charge of walking Steve's proposed engine modifications through the unmapped regulatory jungle.

On June 2, 1988, at Road America in Elkhart Lake, Wisc., Steve announced his intention to sell 250 copies of a street-legal 300-horsepower 1989 Mustang-based supercar in all 50 states. The prototype was a black hatchback, 88-0003, owned by Saleen employee Phil Hubbard, decked out in black DP5 five-spoke wheels and sporting some of the planned engine mods. In July Saleen gave passenger rides in the prototype at Sears Point during a national convention of the Shelby American Automobile Club. The high-speed rides not only generated publicity for the proposed model, but Saleen used the free track time to research and develop a supercar suspension.

Although Saleen liked the purposeful Darth Vader-like appearance of the prototype, his hope to blanket the enthusiast magazines with the new model caused an immediate color change when a photographer pointed out that no editor likes to put black cars on the cover. Not only are they hard to photograph under natural lighting conditions, but there is a long-held belief in the newsstand business that black cars equal death for issue sales. Saleen decided against red, because Ford was making a change to its red paint. White, he felt, had a more subtle appeal that suggested refinement—not just raw horsepower.

The black prototype was called "SA-5," which commemorated the company's fifth year in business, but with the color change came a new name—SSC. Saleen says

The SSC was never intended to be a tire-screeching musclecar; instead, it served its purpose well as a powerful and luxurious two-seater. *(Brad Bowling)*

While in development, the SSC's 5.0-liter V-8 was advertised as producing more than 300 horsepower, but that rating is more likely around 292. *(Brad Bowling)*

Leather was liberally applied to the SSC's interior. *(Brad Bowling)*

he chose "SSC" because it had no meaning whatsoever but sounded racy. Contrary to legend, it does not stand for "Saleen Super Coupe" or "Saleen Super Car."

One month later, Saleen unveiled a white SSC in Boston during a show of Ford's 1989 cars and trucks. It had gained the short yellow and black markings commemorating the Saleen Autosport race team colors and the gray wraparound body molding that would become its signature look.

Saleen's timing could not have been better. There was an angry buzz in the Mustang hobby as the marque's 25th anniversary approached, and Saleen was hearing it loud and clear. It seems Ford had been hoping to kill off the rear-drive Mustang to allow room for more profitable, futuristic designs such as the Taurus and Probe front-drivers; in its haste to pull the plug, it had neglected to create a special 25th anniversary commemorative model. Ford had been developing a high-flow head design known internally as "GT40" during the late 1980s with an eye toward introducing it on a 25th anniversary Mustang model in 1989. Unfortunately, a new set of heads was not enough to push Ford into production of a separate model;

This black SA-5 is the only one of its kind. It was built to act as a development prototype for what became the white SSC line. *(Brad Bowling)*

the GT40 components would be released two years later through SVO's parts catalog.

In the fall of '88, it looked as though a Jack Roush-built Mustang powered by a 400-horsepower, twin-turbocharged 351-cid V-8 was a contender to be marketed in limited numbers as the silver anniversary car, but Ford turned down the idea as unworkable from an emissions and warranty standpoint, leaving Saleen's super Mustang to be the bright star of the season.

For his own wonder-motor, Saleen started with a stock 5.0-liter, added a high-performance air filter, 65-mm throttle body, high-flow heads, a modified Mustang intake manifold, 1.7:1 rocker arms for increased valve lift, and free-flowing, stainless steel headers. A heavy-duty radiator kept the hopped-up V-8 cool, and Borg-Warner's "world class" T-5 five-speed manual transmission was judged capable of handling the increased horsepower and torque. Dress-up features for the SSC engine included polished stock aluminum valve covers, a special engine plenum plate, and Champion sparkplug wires.

When it went into production, Saleen's SSC V-8 was rated at 291 horsepower; it hadn't met the magic 300 mark enthusiasts had hope for, but it did get its EPA certification.

The SSC program started with the performance equipment found on regular Saleen Mustangs, but then added white DP5 wheels; grooved brake rotors; a heavy-duty clutch; an Auburn-built differential assembly with 3.55:1 gears; three-way Monroe Formula GP adjustable shocks; Walker Dynomax mufflers and pipes; 200 watts of Pioneer CD sound; a custom speaker box; flat gray body molding; special pinstriping; FloFit seats, door panels, a Momo steering wheel wrapped in gray leather; four-point interior chassis stiffener (also known as a "rollbar") and a 200-mph speedometer. The new wheels were 16x8-inchers wearing P225/50ZR16 General XP2000s on front and P245/50ZR16s on the rear, making the SSC the first Saleen to be fitted with Z-rated tires.

The stock Ford lower bumper had been painted black so as to create a look of depth behind Saleen's fascia. Steve Saleen was especially proud of the Monroe shock absorber system in the SSC, which used rotating internal valves that were electronically adjustable from the cockpit to shift from soft to firm.

Carrying his supercar concept into the design of the SSC's interior, Saleen worked with designer Scott McDonald to create a "rear sound enclosure." This uniquely Saleen speaker rack turned the SSC into a two-seater, while retaining an area similar to what the rear seat cushions would normally make that could accommodate soft luggage for a trip.

The completed car debuted at Saleen's open house in conjunction with the American Pony Drive on April 17. The SSC's $36,500 price tag—the regular Saleen hatchback retailed for $23,500—and the late start in the model year may have prevented sales from reaching the 250 mark; by the time Saleen stopped production of its emissions-certified supercar, 161 examples had been built. The only published exception to the SSC equipment list occurred on 89-0159, which was built for DP wheel distributor Automechanica with the Mustang back seat in place and a two-point interior chassis brace.

THE FACTS

Model Year	1989
How Many Were Made?	161
Engine	292-horsepower 5.0-liter V-8
Reason for Limited Edition	to launch premium series
What Made It Special?	equipment level, paint, graphics, engine upgrades
Registries/Clubs	www.saleen.com www.soec.org
Books	*The Saleen Book: 20 Years of Saleen Mustangs* (2004, Brad Bowling)

Saleen SC
1990-93

photo car owned by Mark LaMaskin (white)
photo car owned by Bryan Ross (green)
photo car owned by Bill Price (yellow)

Ford's Mustang was fundamentally unchanged for 1990—a driver's airbag and improved front suspension geometry were the most significant improvements—which freed Steve Saleen to continue producing the line of high-performance ponies bearing his name.

Saleen made slight revisions to the Racecraft suspension system, substituting variable-rate front and rear coil springs for the older specific-rate units. The rest of the system included Monroe Formula GP gas shocks all around, special strut mounting bearings, urethane sway bar pivot bushings, and high-performance alignment specs. The aerodynamic body package was improved by a redesigned "split" front air dam, two-piece rear wing, and bolt-on subframe connectors.

Expanding on the supercar program begun in 1989 with the one-year-only SSC model, Steve Saleen introduced a new series of limited edition, premium-performance Mustangs built around the EPA-certified 5.0-liter V-8 engine.

The SC received all standard 1990 Saleen equipment—aerodynamic body components, sporty interior, Racecraft suspension, and such—and the centerpiece V-8 benefited from new Saleen-cast upper and lower intake manifolds and stainless steel headers for a boost to 304 horsepower. Complementing the SC-only engine were Borg-Warner's heavy-duty ("world class") T-5 five-speed manual transmission, stock 3.55:1 rear axle gears in an Auburn-built cone clutch, white or silver 16x8-inch DP five-spoke alloy wheels, P225/50ZR16 (front) and P245/50ZR16 (rear) General XP2000Z tires, three-core radiator, Walker Dynomax mufflers, Champion sparkplugs and wires, heavy-duty battery, 200-mph speedometer, and Saleen SC Edition FloFit Sport Seats.

According to the ID tag in the engine compartment, this SC was built in the Anaheim plant before production was split between St. Louis and Long Beach. *(Brad Bowling)*

All SCs were equipped with Borg-Warner's heavy-duty five-speed transmission. *(Brad Bowling)*

Unlike the SSC that came before it, the SC was available in colors other than white. This one just happens to be white. *(Brad Bowling)*

The $33,990 SC—available as Black, White, or Bright Red hatchbacks only—received the same chassis reinforcements as the basic Saleen Mustang, but the unique intake manifold required a slightly different strut tower brace for clearance. Further setting them apart from their stablemates, the SC body molding was painted to match the rest of the exterior, and two short diagonal stripes at the rear of the front fender and small "SC" lettering on the body molding ahead of the rear tire subtly suggested supercar status.

Although the SC came standard with a Pioneer radio/cassette player with six speakers handling 80 watts over four channels, Saleen did not burden it with the '89 SSC's heavy speaker enclosure. The SC also dropped the three-way cockpit adjustable suspension system from its standard equipment list, but the electronic Monroes could be had with any Saleen for an extra charge. An interior chassis reinforcement bar (rollbar) was available to SC buyers for an additional $600.

In the middle of the production year, slow sales of all Saleen Mustangs forced the company to subcontract its conversion work to an outside firm for the first time in its history. A Cars & Concepts facility in St. Louis, Missouri, began building standard Saleens in August of 1990, while Saleen Performance Parts Inc.—a spinoff of Saleen Autosport located in southern California—was responsible for assembling SCs. Saleen would close out the year selling 243 standard models and 13 SCs.

The arrangement with Cars & Concepts and Saleen Performance Parts remained in place through the end of 1991 production, during which time Saleen sold only 92 standard cars and 10 SCs.

The following season Cars & Concepts closed its St. Louis plant and standard Saleen Mustang assembly relocated back to southern California.

There were several improvements made to the regular and SC models for 1992. Saleen upgraded his line to 17-inch wheels for '92, motivated by the fact that Ford had begun installing 16-inchers to its V-8 Mustangs a year before. The five-spoke Stern alloy wheels measured 17x8 in front and 17x9 in the rear and wore BFGoodrich Comp T/As (225/45ZR17 fronts, 235/45ZR17 rears). Most of the aerodynamic kit was a carryover, but the 1990-91 two-piece rear wing was replaced by the single, pre-1990 design.

Saleen offered a long-awaited Vortech centrifugal supercharger option (including headers) in 1992 that increased output of the standard 5.0-liter to an advertised 325 horsepower and the SC powerplant to an estimated 450. The $3,200 blower was an A-trim unit with five pounds of boost, and 10 of the 17 standard Mustangs Saleen built for '92 were so equipped. There were no takers for the SC

The two-piece Saleen wing design proved to be unpopular with buyers. It only lasted two years before being replaced with the earlier version. *(Brad Bowling)*

This is one of ten SCs Saleen built in 1991. *(Brad Bowling)*

The SC wing was identical to what Saleen installed on its regular Mustangs. *(Brad Bowling)*

The newly available supercharger boosted the SC's 5.0-liter V-8 to an estimated 450 horsepower. *(Brad Bowling)*

The large stripe on the hood would be shared with Saleen's SA-10 anniversary car. *(Brad Bowling)*

model in '92, despite the fact it was available for the first time in a convertible form.

The SC returned for 1993, the final year of Fox production, when Saleen sold 87 base Mustang packages, five SCs and nine supercharged SA-10 anniversary cars. Three of the SCs were $44,490 convertibles; two were $39,990 hatchbacks.

1993 marked the final year of Fox-body Mustang production. The supercharged Saleen SC represents the peak of that platform's development. *(Brad Bowling)*

THE FACTS

Model Year	1990-93
How Many Were Made?	13 (1990)
	10 (1991)
	5 (1993)
Engine	5.0-liter V-8
Reason for Limited Edition	to showcase performance engine
What Made It Special?	equipment level, engine upgrades, optional supercharger
Registries/Clubs	www.saleen.com
	www.soec.org
Books	*The Saleen Book: 20 Years of Saleen Mustangs* (2004, Brad Bowling)

1992-93
SAAC Mk I, Mk II, and Snake

In 1992 Carroll Shelby was working exclusively with Lee Iacocca, Robert Lutz, and Thomas Gale at Chrysler on the soon-to-debut RT/10 Dodge Viper, yet a new Mustang boasting his name was appearing on magazine covers.

No, Shelby wasn't double-dipping the auto industry or cheating his Chrysler contract—the pony in question was produced by the Shelby American Automobile Club (SAAC) as a commemorative model in his honor.

Since its inception in 1975 SAAC has been one of the most active single-marque car clubs on the planet, devoting thousands of man-hours to researching, documenting, and protecting the historic value of Carroll Shelby's Ford-based performance vehicles. Until the summer of 1991, that list included the GT-350, GT-500, Cobra roadsters and coupes (with various 260-, 289- and 427-cid powerplants), and GT-40 supercars. At the SAAC national convention and open-track event at Charlotte Motor Speedway in 1991, Ken Eber and Rick Kopec introduced the club's modern interpretation of a GT-350 in the form of a white Mk I hatchback.

Based on the production Mustang GT, the Mk I featured a 295-horsepower 5.0-liter V-8 (improved through new GT-40 upper and lower intake manifolds), an LX wing, Hurst short-throw shifter, alloy wheels (17x7.5 in front, 17x8.0 in the rear), 245/45ZR17 Goodyear Gatorback tires, suspension upgrades, "SAAC"-branded leather interior, and blue body decals that recalled Shelby's "LeMans" racing stripes. All SAAC Mustangs had five-speed manual transmissions and 3.27:1 rear axles, but buyers could pay extra for 3.55:1 gears.

Like the GT-350 before it, each SAAC car wore a badge stamped with its individual series number in the engine compartment and on the dashboard. The GT's

The Mk II was available in either hatchback or convertible models. (SAAC)

"cheese grater" taillights were replaced with smoother LX units, and the superfluous foglamps were removed. As a nod to the 1965 GT-350 (the model's first year), the Mk I was only available as a white hatchback. The only other advertised option was a Kenwood stereo.

The three Mk I prototypes looked great on the Charlotte track and generated orders for more than two dozen copies. Those demonstrator models and the next six cars were each labeled "Shelby AAC Mk I," but a complaint by Chrysler forced SAAC to drop the "Shelby" mention, resulting in a switch to "SAAC Mk I" badges. Regardless of its true name, the Mk I stickered for $40,000 when a regular GT could be had for less than $16,000, so the 1992 run of 37 units was indeed impressive.

Kopec and friends introduced their planned Mk II for 1993, available in exterior combinations of red/white, red/gold, or black/gold as either a hatchback or convertible. A nostalgic padded two-point rollbar was fitted to each

The GT's upper and lower intake manifold halves were replaced on the SAAC Mk cars by this GT-40 unit. *(Jerry Heasley)*

The Mk I and II were fitted with custom leather interiors. *(Jerry Heasley)*

LeMans stripes and the tri-bar racing lines recalled the GT-350's glory days on race tracks all over the world. *(Jerry Heasley)*

Three prototypes generated interest and sales at the Charlotte SAAC meet in 1991. *(Jerry Heasley)*

droptop Mk II. SAAC also debuted a Snake model that year that was in every way similar to the Mk I and II, but deleted the engine upgrades and leather interior. Intended to be the entry-level SAAC Mustang, the Snake listed for $26,995 as a hatchback and $30,995 as a convertible.

SAAC built 17 Mk II Mustangs and 11 Snakes in '93.

When Ford's own SVT arm introduced its similar Cobra for $15,000 less than the Mk series, SAAC realized it could not compete and ended production at the end of the 1993 model year after creating a total of 65 cars.

THE FACTS

Model Year	1992-93
How Many Were Made?	(Mk I prototype) 4
	(Mk I certification unit) 1
	(Mk I production hatchback) 30
	(Mk I drag car) 1
	(Mk I R-model) 1
	(Mk II prototype convertible) 1
	(Mk II production hatchback) 3
	(Mk II production convertible) 13
	(Snake hatchback) 8
	(Snake convertible) 3
Engine	5.0-liter V-8
Reason for Limited Edition	commemorate original Shelby Mustangs
What Made It Special?	equipment level, engine upgrades
Registries/Clubs	www.saac.com
Books	*Shelby American World Registry* (1997, Editor Richard J. Kopec)

122 • Mustang Special Editions

SVT Cobra R

photo car owned by Jimmy Morrison

By 1993 Ford's Fox-based Mustang had served the company—and the enthusiast community—quite well for 14 years and a group of hardcore faithful worked behind the scenes to create a four-wheeled bon voyage party.

Ford's Special Vehicle Team (SVT) had been created in 1991 with the same mission as the '80s Special Vehicle Operations (SVO) group—to raise the Mustang's performance bar by producing a limited run of factory-blessed supercars. SVT was in charge of marketing, training, and customer-relations chores; another arm, Special Vehicle Engineering (SVE) was devoted to developing and building the final product.

This "thinking outside the Fox" cooperative effort announced the first of two premium performance vehicles in February of 1992 as '93 models. The first model, the Lightning, was based on Ford's popular short-wheelbase F-150 pickup, but with a 240-horsepower 351-cid V-8 and a mess of suspension upgrades never before seen on production hay haulers.

SVT's golden child, however, was a hopped-up version of the Mustang that benefited from many of the go-fast parts already being sold through Ford's existing dealer network.

Deliberation over the name of the new steroid-fed pony was quick and decisive—it would be called "Cobra" after the world-class sports cars Carroll Shelby began producing and selling through Ford dealerships in 1962. Although production barely topped the 1,000 mark before the end in 1967, Shelby's Cobra roadsters and coupes were the cars to beat on the track and on the street for the rest of the decade—leaving everything from Corvettes to Ferraris in their wake.

In 1968, the Cobra name had been applied to Shelby's Mustang-based GT-350s and GT-500s for the first time, as well as to Ford's top-performing V-8 powerplants, where it was used to indicate various 351-, 428-, and 429-cid engines through 1973. In 1976, the model and emblems were revived as a "Cobra II" cosmetic package for the very low-performance Mustang II, a line that culminated with the extremely garish, but no more powerful, King Cobra in '78. A re-design of the Mustang for '79 brought with it another attempt to recall the memory of those early Cobra roadsters—this time as a cosmetic and performance upgrade accompanying the turbocharged four-cylinder or V-8 engines. In 1982, the new GT displaced the Cobra as Ford's performance Mustang, and the coiled snake emblem

Ford's new SVT arm built 107 Cobra R-models for 1993. *(Brad Bowling)*

If the back half of the Cobra R's interior seems strange, it's because all parts of the rear seat have been deleted and the empty area simply covered by carpet. The irregular bulge in the cargo area is created by the full-size spare tire—a necessity because of the R-model's bigger brake discs and calipers. *(Brad Bowling)*

Contrary to popular misinformation, the R-model did not receive any engine modifications. The R's 5.0-liter V-8 produced the same 235 horsepower as the street version. *(Brad Bowling)*

seemed destined to fade into history. (It should be noted that Ford continued using the Cobra name on GT Mustangs sold in Canada from 1984-92.)

The enthusiasts at SVT knew they were planning a car worthy of a revered name, so when the new model was introduced as a 1993, it was unashamedly wearing Cobra badges. During its freshman year the Cobra was available as a hatchback only; its sole powerplant offering was a 235-hp version of Ford's forever-young 5.0-liter V-8. The 30-hp boost over the GT's engine was due to new upper and lower intake manifold designs, revised "GT40" heads with larger intake and exhaust ports, larger valves, and revised rocker arms. Throttle body and mass air sensor size were increased to 70mm and 65mm, respectively, for better flow, and a different cam spec was used. The intake manifold was a special two-piece GT-40 design cast from aluminum. Twelve percent smaller crank and water pump pulleys—a hot rod trick long used by late-model Mustang modifiers—were fitted to the Cobra. Block and heads were cast iron. Redline for the Cobra V-8 was a giddy 6000 rpm, with a

fuel shut-off switch putting a damper on an overzealous driver's enthusiasm at 6250 rpm.

The Borg-Warner T-5 transmission was similar to the stock Mustang component, but with phosphate-coated gears and stronger bearings. A short-throw shifter made for more positive gear changes, and the 8.8-inch limited-slip differential was fitted with 3.08:1 cogs. The driveshaft was made of steel, with a hardened yoke.

Keeping a rein on all that new power were big disc brakes on all four corners—a setup not seen on a factory Mustang since the SVO's demise in 1986. The 10.84-inch front rotors were vented, with single-piston calipers; the 10.07-inch rears were also vented and wore calipers actuated by single pistons. Goodyear 245/45ZR-17 Eagle uni-directional tires were mounted on Cobra-unique 17 x 7.5-inch seven-blade alloy rims. The low-profile tires and lower body ride height gave the Cobra its great handling ability.

The suspension, surprisingly, was set up to ride softer than Ford's stock GT as part of SVT's "controlled

This street Cobra has the optional sunroof panel, which was not offered on the competition-ready R-model. *(Brad Bowling)*

The air conditioning system and stereo equipment were deleted on the R-model. *(Brad Bowling)*

compliance" philosophy. Front components included modified MacPherson struts, with separate springs on the lower arms, 400/505-pounds-per-inch variable rate coil springs, and a 28.5mm stabilizer bar. Underneath the rear of the car is a rigid axle, upper and lower trailing arms, two leading hydraulic links, 160 pounds-per-inch constant-rate coil springs, shock absorbers, and a stabilizer bar.

Despite its higher price tag and high-tech speed parts, the car's body was a fairly conservative package, free of the contrasting stripes and "look-at-me" badges that had adorned the 1980s Cobra Mustangs. The GT's lower grille and bumper were used, but with a slight grille opening sporting a galloping pony. Side-mounted ground effects were smooth from one end to the other, in marked contrast to the GT's boy-racer design. In back was a one-piece fascia with dual stainless steel 2.25-inch exhaust pipes poking out beneath and a square-shouldered wing mated to the hatch lid. Modified SVO Mustang taillights gave the new car a link to its legendary past. If not standing close enough to see the small coiled-snake emblem on the front fender or subtle "SVT" initials just below the rear wing, the average car enthusiast would be hard-pressed to identify the Cobra.

Interiors drew mostly from the GT standard equipment list, differing only in the white-faced instruments that have since been used on all successive Cobras. Cobra drivers could watch the white-faced speedometer reach 60 mph in less than six seconds and a quarter mile in 14.5 seconds, while keeping the tachometer needle hovering around the stratospheric 6000-rpm neighborhood.

With a list of standard equipment including driver's-side airbag, articulated sport seats, Premium Sound, Power Equipment Group, rear window defroster, air conditioning, cruise control, front floor mats, and dual illuminated visor mirrors, the only options were leather seating surfaces, four-way power driver's seat, sunroof (after Feb. 1 build date), CD player, California emissions equipment, and a high-altitude principle-use package. Available only in Performance Red, Teal, or Black, the 1993 SVT Cobra was clearly the pinnacle of the Fox-bodied Mustang platform. To enhance collectibility, each Cobra starting with the

Many enthusiasts purchased the 1993 SVT Cobra R to preserve it as a collectible. This no-mile example belongs to Jimmy Morrison in Concord, N.C. *(Brad Bowling)*

'93 went to its new owner with a signed certificate that documented the car's production number (from SVT) and VIN (from Ford).

Because it was common knowledge by mid-1993 that the Mustang was due for a major re-design within months, writers for the car magazines were curious as to why SVT would put out so much effort for a one-year-only model. Even though no official explanation was forthcoming, the consensus is that Ford wanted to draw attention away from General Motors' new-for-1993 275-hp Camaros and Firebirds.

To take the Fox body out in grand style, a "best of the last" model was officially announced on April 7, 1993, that would turn SVT's Cobra platform into a true race car. Despite a hefty $25,692 MSRP, the entire 107-unit run was claimed just a few hours after Ford began taking orders.

Price considerations and faith in its 235-horse street Cobra powerplant kept SVT from seeking additional ponies under the hood; instead, the engineers tightened the car's suspension and chassis through a multitude of tweaks. Underbody braces from Ford's Mustang convertible were welded to the chassis, and a special triangular brace was installed to prevent flex between the strut towers and firewall. Progressive-rate springs were installed with track time in mind: fronts were rated 750/850 pounds per inch, and the rears were 240/360. Adjustable Koni shocks and struts and fatter anti-sway bars were also employed to give the R its competitive cornering ability.

Race-quality PBR disc brakes measuring 13 inches in diameter went behind the front wheels; the rear axle received 10.5-inch Lincoln Mark VII units. SVT retained the same Goodyear Gatorback tire size for its R-model (245/45ZR17), but specified the new-for-1994 Mustang GT's 17-inch six-spoke wheel design in basic black with a polished stainless steel center cap. Unfortunately for the sake of aesthetics, the street Cobra's 17-inch spun-aluminum space-saver spare tire would not clear the R's 13-inch brake setup, so the car's cargo area carries a heavier full-size unit.

Other R-unique equipment included a much-improved radiator design Ford lifted from its own turbocharged Lincoln diesel powerplant, a "de-gas" tank to eliminate air pockets in the cooling system and separate tiny radiators for oil and power steering fluid.

What makes the R stand out visually is not any form of addition equipment, but its list of unusual factory deletes. Missing from the mix was stereo equipment, air conditioning, power windows, power locks, foglamps, a back seat, and soundproofing material—all of which added up to a weight savings of 130 pounds.

All 107 Cobra Rs were painted Ford's Vibrant Red (ES code) with a tinted clearcoat and had LX seats wearing Opal Grey vinyl/cloth (G6).

Contrary to SVT's stated wishes, many Rs were purchased for collections and never driven, but several found their way onto America's racetracks and competed successfully in the International Motor Sport Association (IMSA) Firestone Grand Sport Series and Sports Car Club of America (SCCA) World Challenge Class B Series.

SVT's goal of selling 5,000 Cobras was all but met by the end of the model year, with 4,993 of its street-spec $18,505 hatchbacks going to new owners.

THE FACTS

Model Year	1993
How Many Were Made?	107
Engine	235-horsepower 5.0-liter V-8
Reason for Limited Edition	to celebrate return of legendary model
What Made It Special?	equipment level, lighter chassis for competition
Registries/Clubs	www.scoa.org www.svtcobraclub.com www.svt.ford.com
Books	SVT Mustang Cobra Recognition Guide: 1993-2000 (1999, Thomas A Shreiner & Peter C. Sessler)

Saleen SR 1994

photo car owned by Mark LaMaskin

Besides being the start of his second decade in business, 1994 was something of a rebirth for Steve Saleen's California-based small-volume car manufacturing company. The high-performance Mustang builder had overcome three years of slow sales, an ancient Mustang platform, a national recession, and personal bankruptcy to bring a dazzling new line of cars to market.

Three Saleen vehicles made their debuts at the Mustang's 30th anniversary show at Charlotte Motor Speedway in April of 1994. Based on the advanced engineering and sporty styling of Ford's SN-95 platform, the trio ran the gamut from "entry level" to "race car with a license plate."

The "V-6 Sport by Steve Saleen" was the most affordable '94 Saleen, a model that applied the company's traditional cosmetic and Racecraft suspension upgrades to a smaller, more economical powerplant. Its standard equipment list would make any young Mustanger proud: a supercharged 3.8-liter V-6 with 220 horsepower, 17x8-inch alloy wheels, Saleen wing, short-throw Hurst shifter, and leather-grained shift knob. At $22,000 the V-6 Sport cost as much as a loaded Mustang GT, but without the high insurance premium. (Even though the Sport seemed like a good idea whose time had come, Saleen was not happy with the program and would end it after 1994. The majority of the 29 Sports sold never had superchargers installed.)

The most obvious SR equipment is this dual-plane wing. *(Brad Bowling)*

Blacked-out tail lamp surrounds were standard equipment on all 1994-95 Saleen Mustangs. *(Brad Bowling)*

Saleen's new front nose transformed the Mustang from "friendly puppy" to "dangerous predator." *(Brad Bowling)*

The SR was a homologation special, which means it was built to qualify for racing. *(Brad Bowling)*

The next new Saleen product was the awe-inspiring S-351, a package that transformed SN-95 Mustang coupes and convertibles into rivals for the Corvette in terms of all-out performance. Starting with a stock 351-cid V-8 from SVT's Lightning pickup, Saleen engine builders added Edelbrock aluminum heads, a roller camshaft and lifters, 65mm throttle body, 77mm mass air sensor, and an EEC-IV engine management system. Behind that potent, 371-horsepower motor sat a heavy-duty Tremec five-speed transmission and 3.27:1 rear axle (3.55:1 gears could be had for another $813).

Later in the year 12 S-351s were built with Vortech superchargers, which boosted the engine's output to 480 horsepower.

Handling improvements came from Racecraft struts and shocks, variable-rate coil springs (which dropped the chassis a total of three inches), urethane swaybar bushings and caster/camber plates. Sitting at the four corners were BFGoodrich Comp T/A radials (235/40ZR18 in front and 245/40ZR18 in the rear) on alloy rims or extra-cost Dunlop SP8000s (255/40ZR18 in front and 285/40ZR18 in the rear) wrapped around Speedline magnesium wheels. Stock Mustang GT four-wheel disc brakes measuring 10.8 inches in front and 10.5 inches in the rear were deemed suitable for S-351 duty, but for real stopping power a $2,188 upgrade to 13-inch grooved front discs was in order.

Saleen Mustangs have always been known for their eye appeal, and the S-351 was no different. The company produced its own front fascia with five pronounced air scoops below the bumper. Side skirts made the car appear lower, and a new rear bumper cover entirely replaced the Ford piece. Blacked-out tail lamp surrounds and a pedestal-mount wing completed the rear transformation.

Interior upgrades included Recaro sport seats (with matching rears), a Saleen shift knob, white-face gauges (including a 200-mph speedo), a Racecraft steering wheel cover and floormats. Optional equipment included a $344 two-point interior chassis brace, $1,125 Speedster package (convertibles only) and $438 dash-mounted twin-gauge pod.

Racing Recaros and four-point harnesses keep driver and passenger in place when on the track. (Brad Bowling)

Airbags prevented replacing the steering wheel with something sportier, but Saleen improved its appearance somewhat with a wrap. (Brad Bowling)

Relocating the SR's battery to the trunk helped distribute weight for better handling. (Brad Bowling)

Magnesium Speedline wheels help the SR perform on a Corvette level. (Brad Bowling)

The Saleen S-351/SR had the largest engine of any Mustang since 1973. *(Brad Bowling)*

A Vortech supercharger boosted the SR's output to 480 horsepower. *(Brad Bowling)*

The S-351 was not a simple bolt-on hot rod. Each car was built from a stripped Mustang shell and required more than 120 man-hours to finish, giving the S-351 the highest level of Saleen-specific content to date and making the coupe's $34,990 asking price ($40,990 for the convertible) seem quite reasonable. Saleen sold 30 S-351 coupes and 14 convertibles in the model's first year.

With an eye toward eventually resuming Sports Car Club of America (SCCA) competition Saleen turned the S-351 into a race-ready homologation special known as the "SR." This "Supercharged Racer" (the unofficial full name) came standard with the 480-horsepower, Vortech-equipped V-8, dual-plane rear wing, carbon-fiber hood, and an Auburn Traction-Loc rear axle with 3.27:1 gears. A race tray replaced the back seat, and the Spartan interior received a four-point rollbar, four-point safety harnesses, and racing Recaro seats trimmed in cloth.

The SR's magnesium wheels were 18x8.5 inches in the front, 18x10 inches in the rear. Dunlop SP8000 tires measured 255/35ZR18 in front, 285/35ZR18 in the rear. Brakes were similarly impressive, with 13-inch grooved discs in front and 12-inchers in back.

In street trim the SR weighed 3,094 pounds—about 186 less than the GT—56% of which was in the nose. Only two of the $59,990 SRs were built in 1994, but that pair would soon lead the way to more racing championships for Saleen.

The Saleen SR was the baddest of the bad Mustangs in 1994. *(Brad Bowling)*

1994 marked the first time Saleen built its own replacement bumper covers. *(Brad Bowling)*

Only two SRs were built in 1994. *(Brad Bowling)*

THE FACTS

Model Year	1994
How Many Were Made?	2
Engine	480-horsepower 5.8-liter V-8
Reason for Limited Edition	homologate for SCCA racing
What Made It Special?	equipment level, engine upgrades
Registries/Clubs	www.saleen.com
	www.soec.org
Books	*The Saleen Book: 20 Years of Saleen Mustangs* (2004, Brad Bowling)

1995 SVT Cobra R

photo car owned by Mike Morrison

SVT's R-model tradition continued with a bang in 1995!

The street version of the 1995 Cobra received only minimal improvements from the previous model, which is understandable considering Ford and SVT had just introduced a new platform in 1994. To expand its line of Mustang-based products, SVT added a regular (non-Pace Car) convertible model to the group, although it was only offered in Black. Ford's much-touted removable hardtop option—never released as planned in 1994—became a Cobra-only package for '95 before production problems killed the program. Only 499 cars were equipped with the $1,825 option. Coupes were restricted to Rio Red, Crystal White, and Black.

SVT's powerful 240-hp 5.0-liter V-8 was unchanged for 1995, its final year of life as a production powerplant. After 28 years of nearly uninterrupted service to the Mustang, the pushrod 302 was being retired; both the Cobra and GT would receive new "modular" V-8s in 1996. Cobra standard equipment included dual airbags, articulated sport seats (with four-way power driver's seat), premium stereo, Power Equipment Group, rear window defroster, speed control, Cobra floor mats, and dual illuminated visor mirrors. Options for 1995 included leather interior, remote keyless entry system, and the Mach 460/CD equipment.

Because the 1993 R-model had cast such a glamour halo over the rest of the Cobra line, SVT immediately began researching and developing another competition-worthy Mustang around the new SN-95 platform. The company's engineers outfitted two prototypes with 351-cid V-8s from Lightning pickup trucks, Tremec five-speed manual transmissions, 20-gallon Kevlar fuel cells, and other track-ready equipment before entering one car in the annual 24 Hours of Nelson Ledges endurance road race. The R-model mule took a beating in the grueling, day-long event before earning a DNF and landing on its roof, but the

Some of the 250 Cobra Rs produced in 1995 actually spend time on the track. *(Brad Bowling)*

The standard street Cobra for 1995 (above) seemed tamed by comparison to the 351-powered R-model. *(Brad Bowling)*

A stock Cobra spoiler sits on the rear of the R. *(Brad Bowling)*

To save money, no special R-model graphics or badges were created. *(Brad Bowling)*

All unnecessary weight was trimmed from the Cobra R, including the regular Cobra's standard foglamps. *(Brad Bowling)*

SVT crew had seen enough to know that 5.8 liters of power in a new Mustang had awesome performance potential.

When SVT announced a limited run of 250 R-models would make its way to dealerships as 1995s—and that only drivers holding competition licenses could purchase them—Ford pre-sold its entire inventory in the first 10 hours. Each car listed for $37,599, which included a $2,100 gas guzzler tax.

The reason for the R-model's incredible appeal was simple: not since 1973 had a production Mustang been available with such a large engine! Emissions regulations had snuffed Ford's enthusiasm for such powerplants in the 1970s, but SVT found a loophole when researching the feasibility of a 351, and it would pave the way for the fastest Mustang in history. Since the standard Cobra's 5.0-liter/302-cid V-8 and R-model's 351-cid V-8 were part of the same "family," emissions certification was easier than if a different powerplant had been chosen. A Ford marine block formed the basis for the super V-8, with a special camshaft, aluminum alloy pistons, forged steel connecting rods, GT-40 heads and lower intake, and specially designed upper intake manifold making up most of the performance gains. Visually topping off the package was a "5.8 Liter Cobra" plate on the intake manifold. The greater displacement produced 300 horsepower.

Much of the 5.8-liter's creation took place on Ford's Windsor, Ontario, line, then the engine was shipped to Jack Roush's plant in Southgate, Michigan for final assembly. SVT dropped its usual Borg-Warner T-5 for a beefier Tremec five-speed, giving Ford's warranty department peace of mind concerning broken gears, and the 3.27:1 rear axle ratio generated neck-snapping acceleration. To increase its performance potential, the R was stripped of unnecessary components, including the air conditioning

Only 250 Cobra Rs were built in 1995. *(Brad Bowling)*

system, radio, rear seat, some soundproofing materials, and fog lamps.

With a full competition suspension in place, the 1995 R-model's interior was not a pleasant place for a Sunday drive. Progressive-rate Eibach springs rated at 700/850 pounds in front and 200/260 out back worked in conjunction with adjustable Koni shocks, firmer bushings, and bigger anti-sway bars to create an uncompromised ride. The '95 R wore the same PBR brakes as had been fitted to the '93 model, but with dust shields removed for improved cooling, and the street Cobra's ABS system was left intact. Visually, the R's proudest statement was made by its wheel—a graceful, five-spoke design that was also very strong due to its "squeeze cast" construction. Each wheel measured 17x9 inches (the largest in Mustang production history) and wore 255/45-17 BFGoodrich Comp T/As.

Other race-duty equipment included a fiberglass hood, 20-gallon fuel cell and radiators for engine oil and power

Standard Cobra headlights were fitted to the R-model. *(Brad Bowling)*

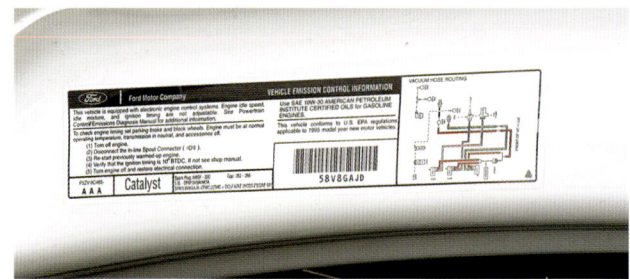
The 5.8-liter V-8 was eligible for Mustang duty because it was part of an approved "family." *(Brad Bowling)*

The 1995 Cobra R's side vent was functional and allowed more air to circulate around the rear disc brake. *(Brad Bowling)*

Part of its weight-loss program was installation of wind-up windows. *(Brad Bowling)*

Figuring they would be replaced with competition-quality pieces, SVT installed Ford's cheapest manually adjusted seats in its R-models. *(Brad Bowling)*

The plain white wrapper conceals an incredibly powerful package. *(Brad Bowling)*

The R-model marked the first time in 22 years that Ford installed a 351-cid V-8 engine in one of its Mustangs. *(Brad Bowling)*

R-model gauges were stock Cobra pieces. *(Brad Bowling)*

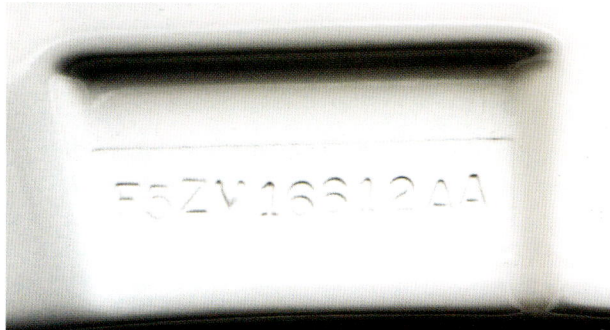
Ford stamped each hood with the VIN of its specific R-model. *(Brad Bowling)*

steering fluid. All 250 cars were painted Crystal White, fitted with the Saddle cloth interiors and built between Feb. 28 and March 2, 1995.

As for Ford's attempt to keep the R on the track and out of the hands of speculators and collectors, the no-mile examples that regularly show up on eBay and through other venues suggest it was an unsuccessful effort. Technically, Ford recorded licensed drivers from SCCA (94 cars), NHRA (86), IMSA (32), IHRA (20), and "other" (18) sanctioning bodies as buying its R-models, but many Mustang enthusiasts sidestepped the competition requirement by asking qualified friends or employees to order for them.

Despite the out-of-the-ballpark R-model sales, overall Cobra numbers were down in 1995. The $21,300 coupe sold 4,005 units and the $25,605 convertible rang up 1,003 new customers.

That bulge in the fiberglass hood was necessary to clear the taller 5.8-liter engine. *(Brad Bowling)*

THE FACTS

Model Year	1995
How Many Were Made?	250
Engine	300-horsepower 5.8-liter V-8
Reason for Limited Edition	just because they could
What Made It Special?	equipment level, special engine, lighter chassis for competition
Registries/Clubs	www.scoa.org
	www.svtcobraclub.com
	www.svt.ford.com
Books	*SVT Mustang Cobra Recognition Guide: 1993-2000* (1999, Thomas A Shreiner & Peter C. Sessler)

2000 SVT Cobra R

Ford pictures

When the SVT crew discovered that a production line change had reduced the potency of its 1999 Cobra by some 20 to 30 horsepower, the high-performance arm of Ford canceled its 2000 output and issued this statement:

The reason for the cancellation is simply that our top priority has been our 1999 Cobra owners. Our focus and resources—and those of our SVT dealers—have been directed to the 1999 Cobra owner notification program. Rather than rushing to produce a limited number of 2000 models—and risking production/manufacturing issues by hurrying—we're choosing to focus our efforts on the timely production of the 2001 SVT Mustang Cobra.

Its recall to address a power deficit in its flagship model was an unprecedented move in the auto industry, but it did not hinder SVT's plans to produce the third in its Cobra R series for 2000.

In assembling an '00 R-model, engineers dug into the modular motor parts bin and tweaked a cast-iron 5.4-liter DOHC 32-valve V-8 until it produced 385 horsepower and 385 lbs.-ft. of torque. The R's 5.4-liter and street Cobra's 4.6-liter share cylinder bore diameters, but the bigger engine's stroke is 15.8mm longer.

A cylindrical air filter by K&N sucks fresh air into a single oval-bore throttle body and 80mm Mass Air Sensor, and aluminum four-valve head work increased airflow by 25 percent. The R-model's exhaust system is made up of stainless steel short-tube headers, a Bassani X-pipe, catalytic converters from the '98 Cobra, Borla mufflers, and dual, twin-pipe side exhausts.

Cradling the pumped-up powerplant low in the engine compartment (a drop of 12mm) are new mounts and a modified crossmember. An extra-capacity Canton Racing Products oil pan filled with synthetic fluid helps keep moving engine parts lubricated on the track. Although a dual-stage rev limiter shuts off fuel at 6800 rpm (and ignition at 7000), redline for the 5.4-liter is an advertised 6500.

Redline for the 2000 R was 6500 rpm. *(Ford)*

The R engine is unmatched for its displacement, generating 71.3 horsepower per liter. This compares favorably to competitors such as the 8.0-liter V-10 Dodge Viper (56.3 hp/liter) and past Cobras such as the 1995 R (51.7 hp/liter) and '99 4.6-liter (69.5 hp/liter).

Shifting all that power is the first six-speed manual transmission ever installed in a factory-built Mustang, a Tremec T56. Behind the Tremec is an aluminum driveshaft and 8.8-inch aluminum-case differential with 3.55:1 gears and induction-hardened GKN halfshafts.

Eibach coils lower the chassis 1.5 inches in front and 1.0 inches at the rear. Brembo four-wheel brake discs, four-piston aluminum calipers, and ducted air inlets make the R-model a powerful and reliable stopper on the street or track. (Ducts were installed only by customer request; otherwise, they were shipped in the car.) The R-model achieved an amazing 1.0g of lateral acceleration, thanks in part to its 18-inch five-spoke wheels fitted with 265/40ZR-18 BFGoodrich g-Force tires.

The street Cobra's dual exhaust cutouts were unnecessary on the R because of its side-exit pipes, so its rear deck and bumper cover were taken from the base V-6 Mustang. Working in concert with the tall rear wing, a specially designed front air splitter worked to reduce lift and increase rear downforce. The splitter also greatly reduced ground clearance, so it was installed by the receiving SVT dealer only at the owner's request.

R-model drivers were treated to racing Recaro seats, a thickly padded steering wheel and a B&M Ripper shifter. As in the past, stock Cobra pieces were deleted to reduce weight: soundproofing material, trunk trim, the spare tire cover, rear seat, air-conditioning, and power seats, to name

Without supercharging, the R-model's 5.4-liter V-8 produced 385 horsepower. *(Ford)*

A side-mounted exhaust system helped reduce weight and increase ground clearance. *(Ford)*

The 2000 Cobra R was the fastest production Mustang in history when it was new! *(Ford)*

a few. The generous standard equipment list included dual airbags, independent rear suspension, ABS, a 20-gallon Fuel Safe bladder-type fuel cell, full-size spare tire, 17-inch rear wing, power dome hood, SecuriLock passive anti-theft system, tilt steering, 180-mph speedometer, leather-wrapped shift knob, Power Equipment Group (no more roll-down windows), dual illuminated visor mirrors, and keyless illuminated entry system.

With zero-to-60 speeds in the sub-five-second range and a top speed north of 170, SVT had no trouble selling all 300 R-models at $54,995.

These 18-inch BFGoodrich g-Force tires were standard R-model equipment. *(Ford)*

Race-ready suspension tuning gave the R 1.0g of lateral acceleration. *(Ford)*

The 2000 Cobra R wore the tallest rear spoiler in Mustang history. *(Ford)*

These racing Recaro seats do little to absorb bumps in the road, but they can hold driver and passenger in place on the track. *(Ford)*

THE FACTS

Model Year	2000
How Many Were Made?	300
Engine	5.4-liter DOHC V-8
Reason for Limited Edition	just because they could!
What Made It Special?	equipment level, special engine, lighter chassis for competition
Registries/Clubs	www.scoa.org
	www.svtcobraclub.com
	www.svt.ford.com
Books	SVT Mustang Cobra Recognition Guide: 1993-2000 (1999, Thomas A Shreiner & Peter C. Sessler)

Roush Boyd Coddington California Roadster

photo car owned by Jimmy Morrison

Jack Roush was not always the guy with the famous name and straw hat coordinating a stable of NEXTEL Cup and Busch Series drivers each week at tracks around the country, but he has long been associated with Fords.

In 1964, the birth-year of the Mustang, 22-year-old Roush started his career as an engineer for Ford Motor Company. After leaving Ford he formed Jack Roush Performance Engineering in 1976 and Roush Racing in 1988. A professional drag racer whose interests eventually led him to success in NASCAR, SCCA TransAm, IMSA road racing, and IRL oval track competition, Roush builds and supplies racing engines for several NEXTEL Cup and Busch Series teams. Roush Industries provides fully integrated engineering and developing support services to the Big Three automakers.

Roush Performance Products, created in 1995, is the corporate arm responsible for the development and sale of high-performance parts and Ford crate engines. To appease his love of performance cars for the street, in 1997 Roush introduced a series of packages for V-6 and V-8 Mustangs to be distributed and—in some cases installed by—Ford dealerships.

The least-expensive of these in 2003 was the $3,875 Sport, which was available on base or GT Mustangs that included no engine modifications. It came with a complete body kit, side-exit exhaust system and a trunk-mounted tool kit, but extra-cost options included a rear spoiler, V-8 suspension (for the base V-6 models) and a brake package.

Next in price and features was the Stage 1, which cost $6,569 when applied to V-6 Mustangs, $6,020 for V-8s. Stage 1 expanded on the Sport components by making the rear spoiler standard and adding a set of 17x8-inch argent wheels and high-performance tires and—on V-6 models—a lowered suspension.

The California Roadster met some North Carolina thunderstorms during our photo shoot. *(Brad Bowling)*

The $9,860 Roush Stage 2 program was applied to GTs only, and included everything in the Stage 1 list plus a performance suspension and 18-inch wheels.

Mustang GT owners looking for more power to go with the improved handling could add $17,645 to the car's factory sticker price by opting for the Stage 3 Sport package. Adding an Eaton supercharger, modified mass-airflow sensor, Bosch fuel injectors, Allied-Signal dual-core air-to-liquid intercooler with electric water pump and recalibrated 4.6-liter computer boosted output to 379 horsepower. The Sport included an aluminum flywheel, sub-frame connectors, 17-inch wheels, a Cobra hood, cosmetic package, and upgraded brakes.

The Stage 3 Rally, for a meager $21,612, built on the Sport components and added a lowered suspension, 18-inch wheels, racing-style metal pedals, and white-face gauges. Finally, the $27,550 Stage 3 Premium package made the standard features list that much longer by including an Alcon brake system and Roush-specific sport leather seating.

Serial-numbered plaques were attached to each of the Series 3 cars to indicate order and year of production. All Stage 3 cars were fitted with fluid coolers when ordered with automatic transmissions.

In 2003 Roush and legendary hot rod builder Boyd Coddington collaborated to produce a special run of 100 one-year-only convertibles built around the Stage 2 and Stage 3 equipment (most noticeably the aerodynamic pieces, sport leather seats, convertible light bar, lowered suspension, serial-numbered plaques, and 18-inch wheels and tires). Known officially as the Boyd Coddington California Roadster, 25 had supercharged 379-horse engines and the rest came with the standard 4.6-liter GT powerplant.

The convertibles were available in red, yellow or silver with black hoods, and the chromed wheels were designed by Coddington, whose signature graces the white-face gauges. Roush charged an additional $11,942 for the California Roadster equipment.

This car is one of 75 California Roadsters built with the stock 4.6-liter GT engine. (Brad Bowling)

Boyd Coddington designed the wheels for this Roush special edition model. (Brad Bowling)

All California Roadster hoods and trunks were black, but the body colors offered were Red, Yellow, or Silver. (Brad Bowling)

THE FACTS

Model Year	2003
How Many Were Made?	100
Engine	4.6-liter V-8, with or without supercharger
Reason for Limited Edition	to collaborate with legendary hot rod builder
What Made It Special?	paint scheme, equipment level
Registries/Clubs	www.roushper.com
	www.thirdgenerationnewsandbeyond.com

SECTION 8:

Fox Limited Editions

It's no secret that the Fox Mustang nearly overstayed its welcome. The 14-year run started strong (we were all grooving to the "European styling" in 1979) and ran hard through the mid-1980s, but ran out of steam in the early '90s.

That's not to say the cars were not good—they were awesome! But just as there is a point at which houseguests and fish must be thrown out, so too should there be an expiration date on most car models. The fact that a 1987-93 5.0-liter Mustang was hands-down the best performance bargain in America would keep the core market buying for decades—running the wheels off their coupes at the dragstrip and coming back for more—but that selling point did little to attract new customers who thought this Mustang looked long in the tooth.

With an all-new design scheduled for 1994, Ford spent as little money as possible on the aged Fox platform, but it did create a quartet of color-based special models in 1990, '92, and '93. All four "Limited Editions" were LX convertibles with 5.0-liter V-8s, custom wheel treatments, and monochrome paint schemes released in the spring and summer months for maximum droptop appeal.

Fox Limited Editions • 139

1990 Limited Editions

Federally mandated safety equipment was the only addition to the Mustang for 1990, including a driver's side air bag and rear shoulder belts. Unfortunately, placement of the air bag meant Ford would not offer a tilt steering column again for several years, and modifiers would be unable to legally change steering wheels on their Mustangs.

The only other change of note was in the form of a missing console-mounted armrest and new map pockets attached to the inner door panels.

Three models were once again available: the base LX, LX 5.0-liter (both of which were available as a sedan, hatchback or convertible), and GT (hatchback or convertible only). The LX 5.0-liter models had the same beefy suspension and tires as the GT, while the GT package added spoilers and an air dam.

Prices for stripped models ran from $9,638 to $18,303, with LX standard equipment including the 2.3-liter four with electronic fuel-injection; power front disc brakes; five-speed manual overdrive transmission; 195/75R14 black sidewall tires; sport bucket seats and a tachometer; plus all the other regular Mustang features. This year, the LX gained the 14.7:1 steering of the previous year's GT and new 14x5-inch stamped steel wheels with turbine wheelcovers.

Special Value Packages enhanced LX base models by adding power locks, dual electric remote-controlled mirrors, power side windows, a premium sound system and speed control (worth $835) for no extra charge. Convertible buyers got the same package free, but it was only a $328 "value" for them, as some of these ingredients were standard on ragtops.

Five-liter LXs ranged from $12,107 for the sedan to $17,681 for the convertible and were equipped with the GT's heftier suspension and bigger tires—but minus the GT's spoiler, skirts and airdam. At the top of the food chain sat the $13,929 GT hatchback (which could be ordered with leather interior trim for the first time) and $18,303 convertible. Clearcoat paint became a Mustang option in 1990.

Between January and April of 1990, Ford produced 4,103 Mustang LX 5.0-liter convertibles wearing monochrome Deep Emerald Jewel Green (code PA) paint schemes, white tops, white leather interiors, Sport Seats,

The 1990 Limited Edition convertible marked the first time the LX 5.0-liter was built with the GT's turbine-blade wheels. *(Peter Sessler)*

trunk-mounted luggage racks, and the GT's turbine-like 15-inch wheels.

Ford officially referred to the model as the "Limited Edition LX," but several other names have been applied to the green droptops that reflect people's opinions about the cars' origin. Urban legend has it that the 1990 LE was Ford Motor Company's way of commemorating the Mustang's 25th anniversary, because each LE had a small tri-bar running horse logo on the dash. This theory does not hold water because a) the Mustang's silver anniversary was in 1989, and b) all Mustangs built between March of '89 and April of '90 wore that dash badge.

The green LE has also been called the "7UP" car and the "NCAA" Mustang, both of which may have some validity. According to Thomas A. Shreiner and Peter C. Sessler's excellent *Fox-Body Mustang Recognition Guide: 1979-1993*, 7UP had a marketing arrangement to give away 30 Mustangs at the 1990 National Collegiate Athletic Association basketball finals to any specially chosen audience member who could sink a basket from center court. According to their sources, the contest was cancelled after Ford had developed the LE package, so the company produced a limited run for public consumption.

Regardless of its original purpose, the 1990 LE succeeded in giving the Fox Mustang an attractive collector model, 1,360 of which were ordered with five-speed manual transmissions. The majority, 2,743 cars, were equipped with the four-speed automatic overdrive transmission. Exports accounted for 261 units.

Ford built 4,103 of these Deep Emerald Jewel Green convertibles in 1990. *(Peter Sessler)*

Ford Motor Company built 128,189 Mustangs for 1990, making it the fifth most popular compact car sold in America despite a nearly 50 percent drop from the previous year.

All Mustangs built between March of 1989 and April of 1990 received this commemorative badge. *(Peter Sessler)*

THE FACTS

Model Year	1990
How Many Were Made?	4,103
Engine	5.0-liter V-8
Reason for Limited Edition	choose your favorite story: 25th anniversary? basketball tie-in? soft drink promotion?
What Made It Special?	paint, equipment level, GT wheels
Registries/Clubs	Feature Car Registry Barry A. Bower 3844 Loren Path St. Joseph, MI 49085
Books	*Fox-Body Mustang Recognition Guide 1979-1993* (2003, Thomas A Shreiner & Peter C. Sessler) *The Official Mustang 5.0 Technical Reference & Performance Handbook* (2000, Al Kirschenbaum)

1990 Limited Editions • 141

1992-1/2 Limited Edition

In 1992 the auto industry was still taking a beating from an economic recession and the slow march of inflation. Ford's Mustang, having gone six years since its last re-design, was generating lethargic sales and another annual price increase. The GT convertible (sticker price, $20,199) had the dubious honor of being the first factory Mustang in history to crack the $20,000 barrier, but four-cylinder models could be had for a more reasonable $10,215 to $16,899.

For their money, buyers of base LX models received a five-speed manual transmission, power front disc brakes (rear drums), and 195/75R14 black sidewall all-season radial tires. Popping for the LX 5.0-liter cost $13,422 for a coupe to $19,644 for the convertible, while stepping up to the GT hatchback ran $15,243.

Changes were few to the 1992, which received some body enhancements including color-keyed bodyside molding and bumper strips, a four-way power driver's seat option, and two new colors: Bimini Blue and Calypso Green.

With no new design or horsepower increase in sight to create excitement, Ford's Team Mustang developed a mid-year convertible package known simply as the "Vibrant Red Limited Edition" (Preferred Equipment Package code 245A). This $850 summer special—similar in concept to the Springtime Sprints of the late 1960s—included an exclusive monochrome Vibrant Red paint scheme, a spoiler produced by American Sunroof (replacing the standard convertible luggage rack) with integrated third brake light, white leather interior with black piping, black headliner, and Opal Pearlescent 16-inch wheels with special "running horse" logo center caps. Cars & Concepts performed final assembly on the package.

All 2,019 LE cars were equipped with the 5.0-liter V-8, and any LX convertible options could be ordered with the Limited Edition, including automatic transmission.

Verifying the authenticity of a 1992 LE is simple, as long as the Vehicle Certification label is intact. Look for an option code of "415," paint code of "EY," and trim code of "CZ." A PEP code of "245A" will also be indicated on the label.

Ford produced 2,019 Limited Edition Mustangs in 1992. *(Jerry Heasley)*

At the end of the model year, only 79,280 Mustangs had been sold. Amazingly, the ancient design remained the fifth most popular compact car in the United States market. Production was split almost evenly between four-cylinder models (36,307 made) and V-8s (36,893 built).

The LE's 16-inch wheels were painted Opal Pearlescent. *(Jerry Heasley)*

American Sunroof produced this unique spoiler specifically for the '92 LE. *(Jerry Heasley)*

All '92 Limited Editions were convertibles. *(Jerry Heasley)*

THE FACTS

Model Year	1992
How Many Were Made?	2,019
Engine	5.0-liter V-8
Reason for Limited Edition	summer sales boost
What Made It Special?	paint, equipment level
Registries/Clubs	Feature Car Registry Barry A. Bower 3844 Loren Path St. Joseph, MI 49085
Books	*Fox-Body Mustang Recognition Guide 1979-1993* (2003, Thomas A Shreiner & Peter C. Sessler) *The Official Mustang 5.0 Technical Reference & Performance Handbook* (2000, Al Kirschenbaum)

1993 Limited Edition

photo car owned by Monty Seawright (black top)
photo car owned by Daniel Carpenter (white top)

The popularity of Ford's 14-year-old Fox Mustang was waning at the start of the 1993 model year. Everyone on the planet had already heard about and seen spy photos of a new, exciting '94 Mustang and only diehard performance enthusiasts were willing to buy a brick-shaped '93 without serious incentives and encouragement.

To make matters worse, Ford quietly announced a 20-horsepower loss for the '93 5.0-liter (from 225 to 205), although the downgrade was purely the result of new dyno testing standards. The final Fox was available in LX, LX 5.0-liter and GT form, and there were the traditional coupes, hatchbacks and convertibles from which to choose.

The base LX coupe, equipped with the same 2.3-liter SOHC four-cylinder we first saw under the hood of the '74 Mustang II, stickered for $10,719 and included a driver's air bag, power brakes with front discs, AM/FM radio with four speakers, reclining low-back bucket seats, five-speed manual transmission, and 195/75R14 steel-belted radial all-season black sidewall tires.

Some '93 feature cars had black tops and interiors. (Brad Bowling)

Moving up to the cheapest performance model presented the LX 5.0 sedan for $13,926 which came standard with a Traction-Lok differential; dual, sport-tuned exhaust system; articulated Sport seats with power lumbar support; constant-ratio power steering; a leather-wrapped steering wheel; a sport-type suspension package; and 16-inch cast aluminum wheels wearing 225/55ZR16 all-season performance tires. Sticker for the LX 5.0 hatchback was $14,710, and a V-8 convertible could be had for $20,293. The new compact disc player was a popular option.

The flashy GT was, once again, available only in hatchback ($15,747) and convertible ($20,848) body styles. In addition to the equipment found on the LX V-8 models, GTs were fitted with a front air dam, foglamps, and color-keyed, flared rocker panel moldings.

To rejuvenate some of the Mustang's lost excitement Ford revived the Cobra name in 1993 on a specialty model produced in-house by Special Vehicle Team (SVT). Built around a tweaked 230-horsepower version of the 5.0-liter V-8, the hatchback-only Cobra came standard with a five-speed manual transmission, 17-inch aluminum wheels, rear spoiler, and ground-effects trim.

Repeating the success it enjoyed with the 1992-1/2 Vibrant Red "feature" model, Team Mustang in collaboration with Creative Industries released two Limited Edition LX 5.0-liter convertibles in the middle of the 1993 production year. The first car, known to Ford by the unromantic name of "Preferred Equipment Package Order Code 415," included Canary Yellow monochrome paint with

Canary Yellow paint really sets this 1993 limited-edition Mustang apart from the herd. (Brad Bowling)

The 5.0-liter V-8 was downgraded on paper for 1993 to 205 horsepower. (Brad Bowling)

black or white top and interior plus chromed, 16-inch five-spoke aluminum wheels for $1,488. The second package, number 201, came with Oxford White monochrome paint with white interior and top and 16-inch painted aluminum wheels for a $976 premium.

Unlike the standard LX or GT convertibles, both LEs wore spoilers on their decklids with integrated center high-mounted stop lights (CHMSL). Headrests were embossed with galloping pony logos, and black floormats came with patterns that matched the car's body. The 1,500 white and 1,503 yellow LEs started down the Dearborn production line on March 1. Potential buyers can verify the authenticity of a suspected LE by reading the metal body buck tag (usually stapled to the radiator support just behind the driver's headlight), which should have the word "FEATURE" stamped on it.

Despite its final-year blues, the 1993 Mustang sold in respectable numbers. 114,228 cars went to new owners, including 4,993 street versions of the new Cobra and 107 race-ready R-models.

The '93 Limited Edition Mustangs were popular "put away" cars. Both photo cars in this chapter had been driven less than 4,000 miles. (Brad Bowling)

Ford produced 1,500 of the white '93 Limited Edition cars. (Peter Sessler)

THE FACTS

Model Year	1993
How Many Were Made?	(white) 1,500
	(yellow) 1,503
Engine	5.0-liter V-8
Reason for Limited Edition	to provide a final special edition to the Fox line
What Made It Special?	paint, equipment level
Registries/Clubs	Feature Car Registry
	Barry A. Bower
	3844 Loren Path
	St. Joseph, MI 49085
Books	*Fox-Body Mustang Recognition Guide 1979-1993*
	(2003, Thomas A Shreiner & Peter C. Sessler)
	The Official Mustang 5.0 Technical Reference & Performance Handbook
	(2000, Al Kirschenbaum)

1993 Limited Edition • 145

SECTION 9:
Movie Tie-Ins

If you think Tom Hanks has an impressive body of work in Hollywood, you should check out a complete bio on Ford's Mustang!

The Mustang must have seen every casting couch in Tinseltown because it has been committed to celluloid as star, support, cameo, and extra. It's been the good guy car (1968's *Bullitt*) as well as the bad guy car (1964's *Goldfinger*). Whole movies have been built around the Mustang, such as 1974's *Gone In 60 Seconds* and 2000's *Gone In Sixty Seconds*. It has been a featured player in many foreign films, taking center stage early in the 1966 French classic *A Man and a Woman*.

Production Mustangs based on movie roles are incredibly rare—the ratio being about 1,000 film/television appearances to every one special edition created—which leads us to believe there must exist a barrier between Hollywood and Detroit.

To date, Ford has only produced one movie commemorative model, 2001's Bullitt, which we review in this chapter. The success and good will it brought the Mustang line ensures that Ford will think long and hard about building a second Bullitt on the fifth-generation platform.

Steve Saleen's creations have also enjoyed screen time—primarily in straight-to-video releases—but that changed in 2003 when three separate big-budget extravaganzas debuted featuring two Saleen Mustangs and an S7 supercar. Not one to miss a marketing opportunity, Saleen produced a limited run of replicas.

2001 Bullitt

photo car owned by Steve Fowler

In 1968 Steve McQueen was a hot property in Hollywood, having just completed *The Thomas Crown Affair* with Faye Dunaway, and he was enjoying the kind of star status every actor works for. Because he wanted more control over the production of his movies, he signed a six-picture contract between his company, Solar Productions, Inc., and Warner Bros. Inc.

The first product of that collaboration was *Bullitt*, based on the novel *Mute Witness* by Robert L. Pike. For the film (in which he plays an unconventional police detective), McQueen envisioned the most violent, realistic, and dangerous chase scene ever attempted. It is a tribute to McQueen's persuasiveness and credibility that the city of San Francisco agreed to the mayhem he proposed creating on its streets. (It's easy to picture the meeting in which negotiations took place, "Okay, Mr. McQueen, you'd like to race two cars through our city at 100 miles an hour—could we interest you in burning down some of our buildings?")

Whether the choice of the Mustang was McQueen's idea or not is unclear; all we do know for certain is that two of them were bought for the movie, both Highland Green fastbacks sporting GT packages and S-code 390/4-barrel motors. Two identical new Dodge Chargers were purchased for the bad guys to drive.

A blacked-out grille treatment was part of the package.
(Brad Bowling)

Bullitt received the stock GT non-functional hood scoop.
(Brad Bowling)

Ford released 5,582 copies of its Bullitt Mustang in 2001. *(Brad Bowling)*

One Mustang was modified with extra welding, bracing, and engine work to handle all of the heavy abuse (the jumping and crashing) while the other was used mostly during the high-speed scenes. Several pieces were removed from the cars, including the driving lights, running pony grille emblem, Mustang lettering and even the GT badges. Stock wheels were pulled in favor of sportier custom-made rims from American Racing.

The modified fastback (the jump car) also received a rollbar-mounted camera so that thrill-seeking moviegoers could get a taste of what it was like to fly through the air above San Francisco's hilly pavement. Not only did that Mustang get trashed performing the jump scenes, but it was also the car responsible for the fiery destruction of the Charger at the end of the chase. Special towing equipment was mounted to the passenger side of the Mustang and two dummies were placed in the Charger so that, through clever editing, it would look like the Mustang ran the Charger off the road into the gas station where it blew up.

Because the main Mustang was so damaged by the time shooting ended, it is highly unlikely anyone at Warner even considered selling it. Most of the people behind the movie recall that it was sent to a junkyard where it was eventually crushed. An editor for Warner Bros. purchased the surviving Bullitt Mustang, which today is hidden in the garage of its third owner, a businessman who prefers to remain anonymous.

In 2000, Ford saw a chance to remind the public how its Mustang had once been chosen by Hollywood to perform in the greatest chase scene ever captured on film by producing a modern one-off Bullitt car for the show circuit. A wave of retro-styled cars (Dodge's Viper, Mazda's Miata, to name a few) had been popular in showrooms, but even Ford was amazed to find Mustang fans panting and drooling at the Bullitt turntable like neighborhood kids chasing after the ice cream truck.

The Mustang GT had become a dominant force and profitable franchise in the performance car market. In 2001 it became a true 1960s musclecar throwback with its pumped-up body and tall (though non-functional) hood scoop, side scoops, a revised spoiler, and blacked-out trim around the headlights. With 260 horsepower, 17-inch

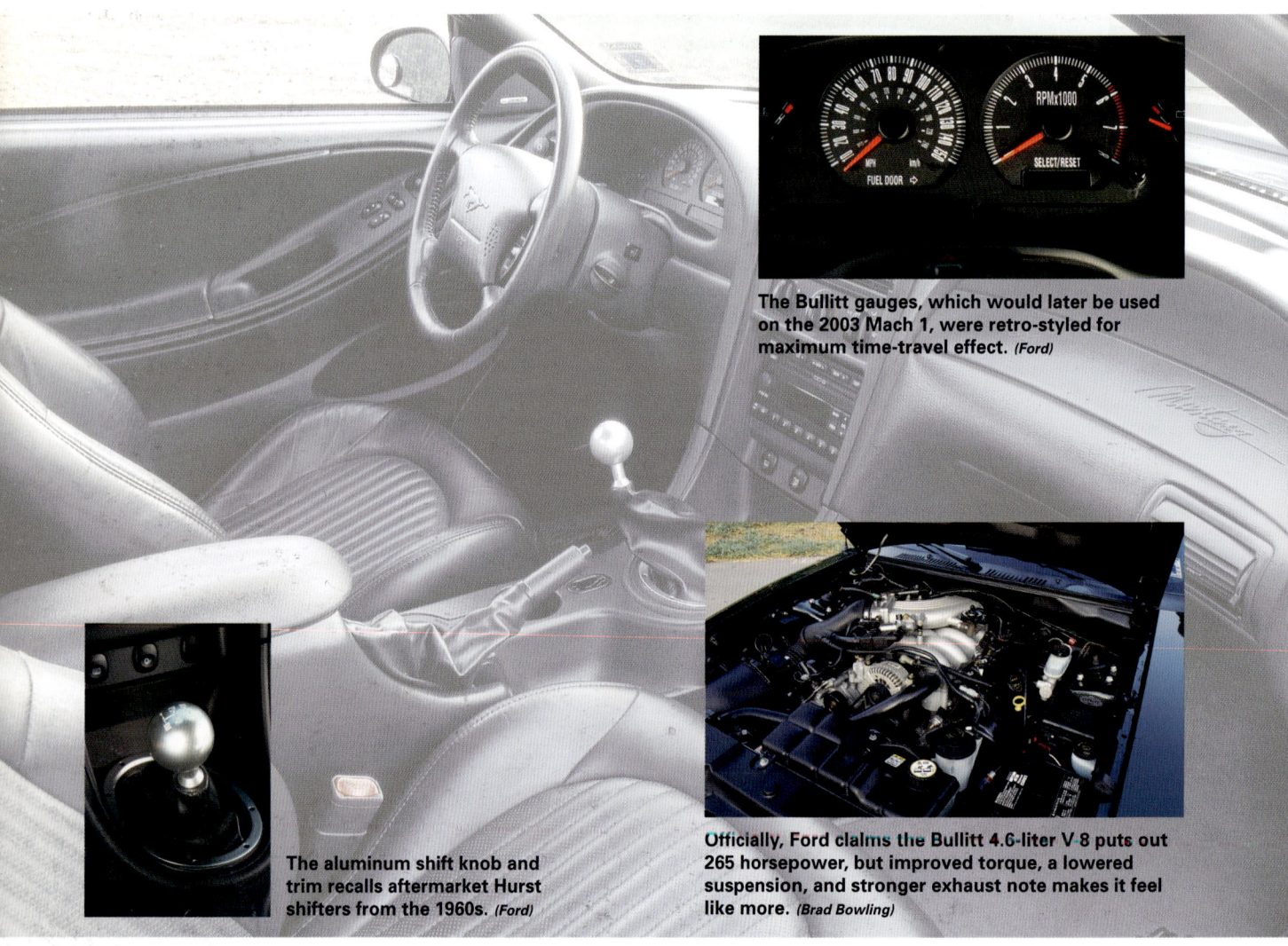

The Bullitt gauges, which would later be used on the 2003 Mach 1, were retro-styled for maximum time-travel effect. *(Ford)*

The aluminum shift knob and trim recalls aftermarket Hurst shifters from the 1960s. *(Ford)*

Officially, Ford claims the Bullitt 4.6-liter V-8 puts out 265 horsepower, but improved torque, a lowered suspension, and stronger exhaust note makes it feel like more. *(Brad Bowling)*

The GT's standard rear wing was deleted when the Bullitt was ordered. *(Brad Bowling)*

No fake side scoops for Steve McQueen! *(Brad Bowling)*

Although they were optional on the GT, these five-spoke rims became known as the "Bullitt" wheels. *(Brad Bowling)*

wheels and a reasonable price tag of $22,630 for the coupe and $26,885 for the convertible, it was every high schooler's dream car and the source of much nostalgia among older fans. Ford marketers knew that combining the already hot GT with a Bullitt package would create an instant collectible.

When Bullitt cars hit the market in early spring of 2001 (Job One was April 10), the limited-edition coupe-only model included unique side scoops, 17-inch American Racing aluminum wheels (copies of that company's Torq-Thrust classic five-spoke), a lowered suspension, modified C-pillars, and quarter panel molding that set the car apart from a stock GT. Rocker panel moldings enhanced the lowered appearance, and a bold, brushed aluminum fuel filler door was prominently placed on the quarter panel. Special Bullitt badging and polished/rolled tailpipe tips further distinguished the car from the regular GT. The Bullitt Mustang was available in Dark Highland Green (PY paint code, 3,041 made), True Blue (L2, 723), and Black (UA, 1,818).

The powerplant was a mildly modified version of Ford's X-code 4.6-liter SOHC V-8, with a twin 57mm-bore throttle body, cast aluminum intake manifold, and high-flow mufflers. Ford itself never seemed to be sure how much power increase there was in the Bullitt package—claims ranged from an early 280 to a more conservative 265 just after introduction—but owners estimate their cars put out somewhere between 270 to 275 horsepower.

Re-valved Tokico struts and shocks, unique stabilizer bars (front and rear), frame rail connectors, and 13-inch Brembo front rotors and performance calipers made up a unique suspension for this special Mustang model. Each of the 5,582 cars came with a unique serialized ID label.

The Bullitt package (code 135A) listed for $3,695 above the cost of a GT for 2001. Ford assured its buyers the model was a one-year-only offering, and that even the Bullitt-specific Dark Highland Green paint was retired from Mustang use.

THE FACTS

Model Year	2001
How Many Were Made?	5,582
Engine	265-horsepower 4.6-liter SOHC V-8
Reason for Limited Edition	to commemorate most famous Mustang movie and its star
What Made It Special?	equipment level, specific engine, unique interior and wheels
Registries/Clubs	www.bullittarchive.com www.imboc.com
Books	*Cars In Films* (2002, Martin Buckley and Andrew Roberts)

2003
Saleen Hollywood Horsepower

photo car owned by Mark LaMaskin

It took Hollywood 20 years to discover Steve Saleen's Mustang and other products, but when the film industry came calling in 2003 the company took full advantage of the exposure with skillfully marketed Hollywood Horsepower limited editions.

Comedian Jim Carrey kicked off the Saleen film festival on May 23 by briefly driving one of the company's S7 supercars in *Bruce Almighty*. Carrey's character assumes the role of Supreme Being after God (played by an ethereal Morgan Freeman) decides to show him it's not so easy running the universe. The newly elected deity's first fantasy fulfillment comes when he turns his decrepit Datsun into a silver S7 and blasts down a miraculously empty city street.

Hollywood's love of quick-money sequels resulted June 6 in *2 Fast 2 Furious*, a follow-up to 2001's *The Fast and the Furious*. Vin Diesel was conspicuous by his absence, but the studio somehow managed to make Paul Walker's payday worthwhile. The real stars of both movies were the cars, of course, and in this respect the sequel did not disappoint its core audience. Shining brightest above the rice-burning "hot rods" were a set of Lizstick Red Saleen S-281s that were eventually destroyed during one of the movie's several climactic action sequences.

Hollywood Homicide, which opened June 13, turned out to be one of the worst movies of the year. Harrison Ford and Josh Hartnett starred in this career-killing mistake in the "old cop/young cop" buddy film genre but the only scenes of any interest were those featuring a silver Saleen S-281 convertible owned by Young Cop.

Despite the questionable quality of the latter two efforts, screen time in three big-budget motion pictures is the kind of publicity that ordinarily costs millions of

Chroming Saleen's 18-inch alloy wheels cost an S-281 buyer $1,119 extra in 2003, but the popular feature was standard on the Hollywood Horsepower package. *(Brad Bowling)*

Can you spot the clues that suggest this is a Hollywood Horsepower commemorative edition? *(Brad Bowling)*

150 • Mustang Special Editions

dollars. To remind moviegoers of its big-screen debuts, Saleen released two S-281 Mustang models in the appropriate colors and body styles just one month before *Bruce Almighty* premiered.

"2F2F" featured a Lizstick Red supercharged coupe, but the cost of that custom color would have limited sales so Ford's Laser Red was primarily used. All 18 red coupes were built with the supercharged 375-horsepower 4.6-liter V-8, and all but two received the 18x10-inch rear tire and wheel upgrades, S-281E-style rear wing, E rear valance, and center exhaust.

The silver convertible S-281 hero car from *Hollywood Homicide* had only been slightly modified when it appeared in the movie. Saleen's standard windshield banner was removed to allow better camera coverage for the embarrassed Ford and Hartnett, but the studio allowed large "SALEEN" graphics to run along the bottoms of both doors so they would be visible and easily read from many angles. For its commemorative model, Saleen returned the windshield decal, but retained the door graphic. Twenty of the 23 *Hollywood Homicide* S-281 convertibles were supercharged, with only two missing the E equipment.

In all, 41 HH cars were built, with Saleen identification numbers running between 03-0264 and 03-0381 (except for 03-0005, which Saleen used as a development vehicle). Because there is no plaque or decal indicating its Hollywood Horsepower identity, it takes a knowledgeable Mustang detective to spot one of the cars sold during that promotion.

Ford dealers encouraged test drives of the special Saleens by offering a free Hollywood Horsepower poster with every visit. After Ford's limited edition Bullitt, Saleen's 2003-only commemorative models proved to be the most popular movie tie-in cars in Mustang history.

Saleen Inc. sold 23 Hollywood Horsepower S-281 convertibles in 2003. *(Brad Bowling)*

The S-281E donated its rear wing and rear bumper cover to the HH series. *(Brad Bowling)*

Twenty-one HH convertibles were built with the S-281E center exhaust feature, but two were shipped without. *(Brad Bowling)*

THE FACTS

Model Year	2003
How Many Were Made?	41
Engines	290-horse 4.6-liter V-8 or 375-horse supercharged 4.6-liter V-8
Reason for Limited Edition	movie tie-in
What Made It Special?	equipment level, paint, graphics
Registries/Clubs	www.saleen.com / www.soec.org
Books	The Saleen Book: 20 Years of Saleen Mustangs (2004, Brad Bowling)

SECTION 10:

The Future Looks Bright!

If you missed the rampant excitement surrounding the Mustang's introduction in 1964, now is your chance to experience it in person! The American public has been so enthusiastic about the fifth-generation Mustang (released late in 2004 as an '05 model) and its retro-1960s styling that Ford exceeded even its wildest sales projections.

Designed to resemble the original 1965 fastback and convertible, the '05 looks as good at 40-plus as it did at its debut. How many of us can say that?

With a 300-horsepower three-valve V-8, a $26,000 price tag, and not a hint of competition in the market, the Mustang GT is poised to maintain its legendary status for decades to come.

In this chapter we review a couple of 2006 Mustang special editions.

(Ford)

2006 GT-500

If novelist Charles Dickens had been alive and working in the early part of the 21st century, he might have written *Great Expectations* about the all-new 2005 Mustang. The eyes of the world were on Dearborn in the summer of '04 to see if the new pony could possibly live up to the buzz; fortunately, the consensus of the industry media and public overwhelmingly declared the '05 to be every bit the second coming of the original Mustang.

Some have referred to the fifth-generation design as "retro," suggesting there is nothing new in its beautiful design. True, the 2005 has the silhouette of a 1965-66 fastback, the rear quarter windows of a '66 Shelby GT-350, wheels from Steve McQueen's 1968 *Bullitt* fastback and grille-mounted lights reminiscent of every GT from 1965 to 1968, but purists see it as four decades of rolling Mustang history. If you ignore the few deep-down chassis parts shared with Lincoln's LS and Jaguar's S-type sedans, it can be argued that this is the very first Mustang created from a clean sheet of paper.

The long, uninterrupted hood is made of aluminum to save weight, and it is balanced on the other end of the car by the traditional short decklid. Where the original Mustang had a strong but friendly look in front, the latest wears the furrowed brow of a predator. Jeweled headlamps sit securely behind clear trapezoidal sheets of plastic, with GT models sporting a set of auxiliary lights in between. Sides have only the slightest indention—a more subtle styling cue than the original's fake scoops—and the rear's three-section tail lamps look as though they've been lifted from a 1970 Mach 1. Ford's designers left behind the "flying wedge" shape that defined the 1994-04 Mustangs, forming the new coupes and convertibles into upright, powerful bricks. Strangely, the

The SVT rear treatment is cleaner and sportier than that on the Mustang GT. (Ford)

The heart of the beast is this 5.4-liter supercharged V-8. (Ford)

The 19-inch wheels on this prototype will be replaced by 18-inchers in production. (Ford)

The family resemblance is difficult to ignore. (Ford)

This side-by-side comparison shows the different grille and bumper treatments between the GT-500 and GT. *(Ford)*

Carroll Shelby, creator of the original GT-500, introduced SVT's new version at the New York Auto Show. *(Ford)*

new model does not look substantially different in exterior size from the 1994-04, but 5.8 more inches separate the front wheels from the rear (for a 107.1-inch wheelbase) and Ford added 4.4 inches overall (187.6 inches).

Inside are state-of-the-art accommodations capable of transporting a driver and passenger in nostalgic bliss for long trips, but attempting to force tall adults into the back seat will lead to mutiny in no time. The dashboard combines 1960s styling with 21st century materials in an eye-catching platform that efficiently houses all necessary gauges and some generous chrome-ringed air vents. Ford enjoyed touting its color-changing gauge option that allows drivers to scroll through 125 different background colors. (The company offers a long, technical explanation as to just how this works but we will skip that lecture.) Front bucket seats seem to sit low in the new Mustang (it's an illusion created by the rather high door sill); they work well for spirited driving but need more side support before taking to the track. A center console sits higher than in years past, and the short-throw shifter has been relocated rearward a few inches to accommodate drivers with shorter arms. If the small, round center of the padded steering wheel did not plainly advertise "AIRBAG" on its surface, no one would guess it had such a device.

To say that Mustang engine choices remain a V-6 and a V-8 sounds as if little has changed since 1994, but nothing could be farther from the truth. Back in the early Clinton era, the base Mustang engine was a 3.8-liter, 145-horsepower V-6 and the GT sported a 215-horse 5.0-liter V-8—both of which actuated their valves by way of buried camshafts and pushrods. The 2005 powertrain lineup includes an iron-block 4.0-liter, 210-horsepower V-6 with single overhead camshafts, and a rip-snortin' aluminum 4.6-liter with three-valve heads and overhead cams rated at 300 horsepower! The GT's block was first seen in the 1996-02 SVT Cobra, and Ford's F-150 pickup supplied the heads.

The base V-6 is fitted with a Tremec T-5 five-speed manual unless the extra-cost 5R55S five-speed automatic is ordered. By default, GT buyers get a Tremec 3650 five-speed manual, but they can pay more for the 5R55S. Live axles supported by a three-link suspension and tubular Panhard bar house either 3.31:1 (V-6) or 3.55:1 (V-8) rear gears.

Four-wheel disc brakes are standard on all '05 Mustangs. Base cars receive 11.4-inch ventilated rotors in front and 11.8-inch solid units in the rear. GTs wear the largest ventilated rotors in production Mustang history—12.4-inchers in front and 11.8-inch units in back. Four-channel anti-lock braking is optional on V-6 cars, standard on GT models.

Standard Mustang safety features include Beltminder (the annoying chime), SecuriLock Passive Anti-Theft System (the chip in the key), a battery saver that turns off lights anywhere from 10 to 40 minutes after the engine stops and fail-safe cooling, which allows the car to limp home on half power if coolant is determined to be critically low.

As is Ford's recent habit, buying a 2005 Mustang is a path of either/or decisions: Either the coupe or convertible (introduced in spring of '05); either the V-6 or V-8; either the manual or automatic; either Deluxe or Premium trim packages.

The V-6 Deluxe comes standard with remote keyless entry, rear window defroster, stainless steel single exhaust, dual power side mirrors, 16-inch painted cast aluminum wheels, air conditioning, AM/FM stereo with single CD player, center console, front floor mats, door map pockets, cloth front bucket seats with 50/50 split rear bench (coupe), tilt steering wheel with speed control, power windows and door locks, front airbags and LATCH system child seat mounts in rear outboard seats. In coupe form, the Deluxe costs $19,890; as a convertible, $24,615.

The V-6 Premium package adds 16-inch bright machined aluminum wheels with chrome spinners, Shaker 500 audio system with six-disc CD changer and MP3 compatibility, six-way power adjustable driver seat, and leather seating surfaces. Premium coupes run for $20,765, and convertibles retail for $25,490.

Ordering a GT Deluxe Mustang brings ABS with traction control, stainless steel dual exhaust, front fog lamps in the grille, complex reflector halogen headlamps with integral turn signals, rear spoiler, 235/55ZR17 tires, 17-inch machined cast aluminum wheels, AM/FM stereo with single CD, cloth sport bucket seats, and leather-wrapped tilt steering wheel. A GT Deluxe coupe stickers for $25,815, while the convertible goes for $30,240.

Above and beyond the GT Deluxe, the Premium adds a Shaker 500 Audio system with six-disc CD player and Aberdeen leather-trimmed embossed sport bucket seats. The top-of-the-line coupe retails for $26,995; as a convertible it sells for $31,420.

There was no SVT-produced Mustang model built in 2005, and as of press time there is no immediate plan to return the Cobra model to production. There is, however, an ultra-high performance SVT model scheduled for a 2006 rollout.

A genuine "blast from the past" by anybody's account, the new GT-500 represents the kind of marriage all automakers dream about—high technology and a nostalgic nameplate that touches the heart of every performance enthusiast. So far, only a bright red GT-500 coupe prototype has made the rounds of the international car shows, but SVT insists the version it is developing for the public will not be substantially different. With an estimated sticker price of $39,000 the '06 GT-500 costs about $34,000 more than the 1967-70 big-block Shelbys did when new, but those cars now bring more than $100,000 each at auction and through private sales.

Because the fifth-generation Mustang is so clearly the reincarnation of the original pony, it only makes sense that the SVT bears a strong family resemblance to the first GT-500. Of course, the prototype wears the necessary coloring—a white tri-bar runs along the bottom of the doors and twin "LeMans" stripes bisect the car from bumper to bumper—but it's the lowered stance, aggressive grille treatment and 1960s-era kicked-up spoiler that give all who see it an emotional sense of *deja vu*.

Should the car's Shelby-esque looks fail to win over Mustang purists (how could it?), the monstrous powerplant that hides beneath the bulging hood should do the trick.

The heart of the new GT-500 is an iron-block 5.4-liter V-8 with double overhead camshafts, four valves per cylinder, an Eaton Roots-type blower, and air-to-liquid intercooler that produces an estimated 475 horsepower. Shifting is handled by a Tremec six-speed manual transmission, which feeds all that power to a limited-slip differential with 3.31:1 gears. Unlike the prototype (which wore 19-inch wheels and 255/45-19 tires all around), the street version of the GT-500 will get around on 18x9.5-inch rims shod with Goodyear Eagle F1 Supercar tires measuring 255/45-19 in front and a massive 285/40-19 in the rear.

The all-wheel disc brake system leapfrogs the Mustang GT's standard equipment by adding 14-inch vented front rotors with four-piston calipers and 11.8-inchers in the rear.

With this kind of equipment and style, if history is destined to repeat itself we will keep listening!

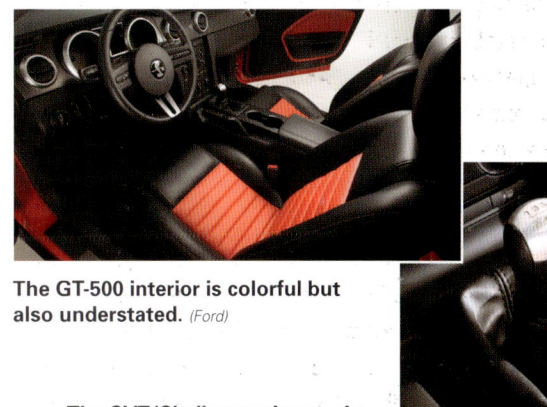

The GT-500 interior is colorful but also understated. *(Ford)*

The SVT/Shelby receives a six-speed Tremec transmission. *(Ford)*

THE FACTS

Model Year	2006
How Many Were Made?	n/a
Engine	5.4-liter DOHC supercharged V-8
Reason for Limited Edition	commemorate Carroll Shelby's original GT-500
What Made It Special?	equipment level, famous name, insane power levels
Web sites	www.scoa.org
	www.svtcobraclub.com
	www.svt.ford.com

2006 Stallion

Not only does the fifth-generation Mustang physically resemble its ancestors from the mid-1960s, it has also recreated the waves of genuine enthusiasm that greeted the 1965 model. As the final chapter of this book is being written, the Flat Rock, Mich., AutoAlliance International plant is operating at full capacity, turning out 70 percent more 2005 Mustangs than Ford anticipated. The new Mustang dominates the sport coupe segment of the American market with a 44 percent share—that's up against popular competitors from Pontiac (the GTO), Nissan (350Z), and Chrysler (Sebring).

Since the earliest spy photos, the new Mustang attracted the attention of designer and musclecar enthusiast Chip Foose. Most couch potatoes will recognize Foose as the customizing artist who turns "stolen" project cars into rolling masterpieces on the TLC cable show *Overhaulin'*, but few realize the Art Center College of Design honors graduate spent eight years under the tutelage of street rod legend Boyd Coddington before creating Foose Design in Huntington Beach.

Working with Dallas-based Unique Performance—the folks that brought the GT-500E Mustang and other "continuation" Shelby models to life—Foose designed an appearance/performance model around the fifth-gen Mustang.

The Foose "Stallion" prototype debuted at the 2005 Woodward Dream Cruise in Detroit to great reviews. Its body modifications include a hood whose power bulge and scoop recall the 1970 Mach 1, special molding that smoothes and appears to lower the side of the car, a billet

A billet grille gives the Stallion an industrial look. *(Jerry Heasley)*

Foose identification is located in several spots around the Stallion. *(Jerry Heasley)*

Chip Foose designed his own 20-inch rims for the Stallion. *(Jerry Heasley)*

The Foose Stallion is scheduled for 2006 release. *(Jerry Heasley)*

Starting with the Mustang's stock 300-horsepower three-valve V-8, the Stallion gains a free-flowing air filter and high-flow exhaust system. *(Jerry Heasley)*

grille that continues into the new front bumper cover, a Shelby-style C-pillar duct, an extended rear spoiler, and custom graphics using duPont's Hot Hues finishes.

Foose designed his own set of 20-inch aluminum wheels for the Stallion, which wear BFGoodrich g-Force T/A KDW ultra high-performance tires. The new pony's four-piston Baer brake system includes Eradispeed cross-drilled rotors measuring 15 inches in the front and 14 in the

The Stallion hood strongly resembles the one found on a '70 Mach 1. *(Jerry Heasley)*

Chip Foose cleaned up the rear of the Mustang when creating his Stallion. *(Jerry Heasley)*

Eibach springs make the Stallion sit low. *(Jerry Heasley)*

rear. A lowered stance and improved handling come from Eibach springs, front and rear anti-sway bars, billet trailing arms, and a strut tower brace.

Although no specific engine modifications have been announced, the Stallion's stock 4.6-liter three-valve V-8 gets help breathing with a high-flow air filter and a JBA high-flow cat-back exhaust with low-restriction mufflers.

The interior benefits from a brushed-aluminum treatment and custom leather seats. Distinctive Foose badges are located in several places around the Stallion. Sequential taillights are optional.

Foose and Unique intend to sell 3,000 of the serialized Stallions through 85 Ford dealerships with a full factory warranty in 2006. Prices are expected to range from $38,000 to $41,000.

Stainless steel trim wakes up the Stallion's interior. *(Jerry Heasley)*

THE FACTS

Model Year	2006
How Many Were Made?	press material predicts 3,000
Engine	4.6-liter SOHC V-8
Reason for Limited Edition	to highlight Chip Foose's design talent
What Made It Special?	modified bodywork, custom wheels, designer panache
Web sites	www.chipfoose.com www.uniqueperformance.com

Mustang Engines

Size (cid/liters)	Type	Bore/Stroke	Carb.	Compression	HP	Years
FOUR-CYLINDER						
140/2.3	I-4	3.78x3.13	2V	8.4:1	88	74-78
140/2.3	I-4	3.78x3.13	2V	9.0:1	88	79-86
140/2.3	I-4	3.78x3.13	EFI	9.0:1	90	87-93
140/2.3 Turbo	I-4	3.78x3.13	2V	9.0:1	131	79-80
140/2.3 Turbo	I-4	3.78x3.13	EFI	8.0:1	145	83-84
140/2.3 Turbo	I-4	3.78x3.13	EFI	8.0:1	175	84-85
140/2.3 Turbo	I-4	3.78x3.13	EFI	8.0:1	205	85
140/2.3 Turbo	I-4	3.78x3.13	EFI	8.0:1	200	86
I-6						
170/2.8	I-6	3.50x2.94	1V	8.7:1	101	64
200/3.3	I-6	3.68x3.13	1V	9.2:1	120	65-67
200/3.3	I-6	3.58x3.13	1V	8.8:1	115	68-69
250/4.0	I-6	3.68x3.91	1V	9.0:1	155	68-70
200/3.3	I-6	3.68x3.13	1V	8.7:1	120	70
250/4.0	I-6	3.68x3.91	1V	9.0:1	145	71
250/4.0	I-6	3.68x3.91	1V	8.0:1	95	72-73
200/3.3	I-6	3.58x3.13	1V	8.6:1	85	79-82
V-6						
171/2.8	V-6	3.66x2.70	2V	8.7:1	109	74-78
171/2.8	V-6	3.66x2.70	2V	8.7:1	109	79
232/3.8	V-6	3.80x3.40	2V	8.7:1	105	83
232/3.8	V-6	3.80x3.40	CFI	8.7:1	120	83-86
232/3.8	V-6	3.80x3.40	TPI	9.0:1	145	94-98
232/3.8	V-6	3.80x3.40	EFI	9.36:1	190	99-04
245/4.0	V-6	3.95x3.32	EFI	9.7:1	210	05-06
V-8						
255/4.2	V-8	3.68x3.00	2V	8.8:1	119	80-81
255/4.2	V-8	3.68x3.00	2V	8.2:1	120	82
260/4.3	V-8	3.80x2.87	2V	8.8:1	164	64
281/4.6 SOHC	V-8	3.55x3.54	EFI	9.0:1	215	96-98
281/4.6 DOHC Cobra	V-8	3.55x3.54	EFI	9.85:1	305	96-98
281/4.6 SOHC	V-8	3.55x3.54	EFI	9.0:1	260	99-04
281/4.6 SOHC Roush	V-8	3.55x3.54	EFI	9.0:1	360-379	99-04
281/4.6 DOHC Cobra	V-8	3.55x3.54	EFI	9.85:1	320	99-01
281/4.6 SOHC Bullitt	V-8	3.55x3.54	EFI	9.0:1	265	01
281/4.6 SOHC Saleen S-281E	V-8	3.55x3.54	EFI	9.0:1	425-445	02-04
281/4.6 DOHC Mach 1	V-8	3.55x3.54	EFI	10.1:1	305	03
281/4.6 DOHC Cobra	V-8	3.55x3.54	EFI	8.5:1	390	03-04
281/4.6 SOHC	V-8	3.55x3.54	EFI	9.8:1	300	05-06
289/4.7	V-8	4.00x2.87	4V	9.0:1	210	64-65
289/4.7	V-8	4.00x2.87	4V	10.5:1	271	64-66 (Hi-Po)
289/4.7	V-8	4.00x2.87	4V	10.5:1	306	65-66 (GT-350)
289/4.7	V-8	4.00x2.87	4V	10.0:1	225	65-66

Size (cid/liters)	Type	Bore/Stroke	Carb.	Compression	HP	Years
V-8 (cont.)						
289/4.7	V-8	4.00x2.87	2V	9.3:1	200	65-67
289/4.7	V-8	4.00x2.87	4V	9.8:1	225	67
289/4.7	V-8	4.00x2.87	4V	10.0:1	271	67
289/4.7	V-8	4.00x2.87	2V	8.7:1	195	68
302/5.0	V-8	4.00x3.00	4V	10.0:1	230	68
302/5.0	V-8	4.00x3.00	4V	10.5:1	250	68 (GT-350)
302/5.0	V-8	4.00x3.00	2V	9.5:1	220	69-70
302/5.0	V-8	4.00x3.00	4V	10.6:1	290	69-70
302/5.0	V-8	4.00x3.00	2V	9.0:1	210	71
302/5.0	V-8	4.00x3.00	2V	8.5:1	136	72-73
302/5.0	V-8	4.00x3.00	2V	8.0:1	122	75-76
302/5.0	V-8	4.00x3.00	2V	8.4:1	139	77-78
302/5.0	V-8	4.00x3.00	2V	8.4:1	119	79
302/5.0	V-8	4.00x3.00	2V	8.3:1	157	82
302/5.0	V-8	4.00x3.00	4V	8.3:1	175	83-84
302/5.0 AOD	V-8	4.00x3.00	CFI	8.3:1	165	84
302/5.0	V-8	4.00x3.00	4V	8.3:1	210	85
302/5.0 AOD	V-8	4.00x3.00	CFI	8.3:1	165	85
302/5.0 AOD	V-8	4.00x3.00	CFI	8.3:1	180	85
302/5.0	V-8	4.00x3.00	EFI	9.2:1	200	86
302/5.0	V-8	4.00x3.00	EFI	9.0:1	225	87-92
302/5.0 Saleen SSC/SC	V-8	4.00x3.00	EFI	9.0:1	292	89-93
302/5.0	V-8	4.00x3.00	EFI	9.0:1	205	93
302/5.0 Cobra	V-8	4.00x3.00	EFI	9.0:1	235	93
302/5.0	V-8	4.00x3.00	EFI	9.0:1	215	94-95
302/5.0 Cobra	V-8	4.00x3.00	EFI	9.0:1	240	94-95
330/5.4 DOHC Cobra R	V-8	3.55x4.17	EFI	9.6:1	385	00
351/5.8	V-8	4.00x3.50	2V	9.5:1	250	69-70
351/5.8	V-8	4.00x3.50	4V	10.7:1	290	69
351/5.8	V-8	4.00x3.50	4V	11:1	300	70
351/5.8	V-8	4.00x3.50	2V	9.0:1	240	71
351/5.8	V-8	4.00x3.50	4V	10.7:1	285	71
351/5.8	V-8	4.00x3.50	4V	11:1	330	71 (HO)
351/5.8	V-8	4.00x3.50	4V	8.6:1	280	71 (CJ)
351/5.8	V-8	4.00x3.50	2V	8.6:1	168	72-73
351/5.8	V-8	4.00x3.50	4V	8.8:1	NA	72
351/5.8	V-8	4.00x3.50	4V	8.6:1	275	72
351/5.8 Saleen S-351	V-8	4.00x3.50	EFI	9.0:1	400	94-99
351/5.8 Cobra R	V-8	4.00x3.50	4V	9.0:1	300	95
390/6.4	V-8	4.05x3.78	4V	10.5:1	320	67, 69
390/6.4	V-8	4.05x3.78	4V	10.5:1	325	68
390/6.4	V-8	4.05x3.78	2V	10.5:1	280	68
428/7.0	V-8	4.13x3.98	4V	10.5:1	355	67 (GT-500)
428/7.0	V-8	4.13x3.98	4V	11.6:1	360	68 (GT-500)
428/7.0	V-8	4.13x3.98	4V	10.6:1	335	68-70 (SCJ)
429/7.0	V-8	4.36x3.59	4V	10.5:1	375	69-70 (HO)
429/7.0	V-8	4.36x3.59	4V	11.3:1	370	71 (CJ)
429/7.0	V-8	4.36x3.59	4V	11.3:1	370	71 (CJ-RA)
429/7.0	V-8	4.36x3.59	4V	11.3:1	375	71